# Coyote Tales
## of the
## Northwest

**Thomas George**

ESCHIA
BOOKS

VILNA LIBRARY

The Publisher: Eschia Books Inc.

Library and Archives Canada Cataloguing in Publication

George, Thomas, 1977–
Coyote tales of the northwest/ Thomas George.

ISBN 978-1-926696-09-6

1. Coyote (Legendary character)—Legends. 2. Indians of North
America—Folklore. I. Title.

E98.F6G36 2010          398.2089'97          C2010-904082-1

*Project Director:* Kathy van Denderen
*Cover Image:* © Candyspics | Dreamstime.com (painted sky
texture); © Hemera Technologies and © Jupiterimages
(all other paint textures)

We acknowledge the support of the Province of Alberta
through the Alberta Foundation for the Arts.

We acknowledge the support of the Canada Council for
the Arts which last year invested $20.1 million in writing and
publishing throughout Canada.

*Nous remercions de son soutien le Conseil des Arts du Canada,
qui a investi 20,1 millions de dollars l'an dernier dans les lettres
et l'édition à travers le Canada.*

Canada Council    Conseil des Arts
for the Arts      du Canada

*To the tribes in Interior/Salish, BC, and Washington, and to my editor, Kathy, for her deft handling of these stories.*

# Contents

# Foreword

ALTHOUGH THESE STORIES ARE easily accessible, they are more than simple entertainment for the reader. The stories represent a belief system and a way of interacting with the world long since past. But the message within each story will resonate through time because the themes are universal to the human condition. We all seek to understand the world around us, and these stories are a culture's attempt at making sense of the world.

# Introduction

IN MANY WAYS, WE HAVE lost our ability to look upon the world as a place of magic and wonder. Science has decoded the very essence of our humanity, and looking to the stars, we no longer have to wonder how things came to be. But long ago, to the Native peoples of the Northwest Interior of North America, the earth and the stars were the domain of great powerful spirits and fanciful magic. We might believe that it was the Big Bang that was responsible for the creation of the universe and all that is within, but in some ways, I almost prefer the stories I heard as a child, in which the Great Spirit creates the universe with just a thought and Coyote wanders the newborn earth creating all the animals and people.

Generation after generation, stories much like these have been passed along as a means of preserving a shared history and culture. Storytelling was a tribe's most ancient pastime and remains the people's oldest possession. Oral stories were the tribe's literature, histories and memories of a time long since passed. The tales were as wide in their character as the experiences of the people. The stories told of travels to distant lands, adventures in unknown places and discoveries never before seen. In the stories lived the heroes and villains and the tales that carried the lessons and morals of a rich culture. These were simply stories, but their beauty and poetry were not lost on the people.

The character that was most popular and important was Coyote because it was he who was put on earth by the Great Spirit to make the world a good place to live for all creatures big and small. But for all the good that he did, Coyote was also known as a cunning trickster who amused himself often at the expense of others.

In this storytelling tradition, Coyote has been around from the beginning of time and will forever exist. You might find in some of the stories that those characters close to Coyote act as if interchangeable; this is because Coyote has lived many lives over the millennia, given life to many children and had many different wives. Time has no meaning for Coyote because he exists outside its boundaries. In this manner, the character of Coyote in one story might be kind and compassionate, while in another his lustful eye might get him into trouble. One thing is certain, though. Coyote could always be counted on to provide entertainment, and the stories in this book show some of the good and some of the mischief that Coyote is well known for.

It is with an imagination of a child that I hope you enjoy reading these stories and open your mind to another world. And the next time you look up at the stars, you might just see something you never imagined possible.

# The Four Creations

### One

THE STORY OF THE FIRST creation began long ago when the lands were dark, for there was no sun and no moon in the sky. The earth was barren but not devoid of life because there was always Coyote.

Coyote lived a lonely existence, walking along through the dark with no one to talk to or be his companion. He sometimes ran into his brother Fox and the pest Raven, but for the most part, Coyote lived a solitary life, scavenging food along the shores of the mighty Fraser River. Coyote was unhappy with this state of existence.

Then the Great Spirit created the sun and the moon, bringing light unto the world. Coyote saw the beauty of the world for the first time but was not moved by its splendor because he had no one with which to share the experience. So he continued to walk the earth in a sad state. Seeing this, the Great Spirit decided to make Coyote a wife.

When Coyote returned from one of his hunts, he found a beautiful woman waiting for him inside his home. They immediately fell in love and got married. Coyote was finally content with his life, and every day when he woke up, he would turn over and tell his wife how much he cared for her.

One day while Coyote was out searching for food, the Great Spirit paid him a visit and told him that although he now had a wife, a day would come when she would die because she did not possess magic and could not live throughout eternity.

Coyote grieved for days over the news and decided not to tell his wife of her fate. For many years, Coyote and his wife lived in happiness. But as time passed, Coyote's wife grew old while he remained as young as the day they met. Seeing his wife age made Coyote very sad, but he still did not tell her of her fate.

But all things must pass. One morning as Coyote woke to greet the sun, he realized that his wife had not woken from her slumber. She had died during the night. Even though Coyote knew that his wife would one day die, he still wept tears that he continues to shed without end. He cried so many tears that he created the great river, the Columbia. It is said that when the river is high, Coyote is thinking of his love.

Coyote wandered the beautiful mountains and valleys, the image of his wife never once leaving his mind. The Great Spirit created many more beautiful young maidens for Coyote, and although he lived with them and had children with them, it just was not the same. His children grew up big and strong, spreading across the earth, but still Coyote mourned his wife's loss and was angry with the Great Spirit. As his children were an extension of Coyote's life, they too inherited the same frustration with existence and carried that feeling into generation after generation. The world became a place of war and strife. The Great Spirit saw the misery and despair of the people and could not continue along this path.

"Coyote has passed on malice and despair to the world, and the people have gone off the path that I chose for them," said the Great Spirit. And with that thought, the earth turned over, and everything began anew.

## Two

And there was Coyote. Coyote has always existed and will forever exist. This was a time when the lands were very dry and hot because Sun refused to set. Life was difficult for Coyote, as he did not like the heat, so he spent most of his days sitting under a tree in the shade.

Coyote had become bored with this existence and decided to create people. He took some mud from the edge of the great river and formed them into people, but under the brutal tyranny of Sun, the mud dried and the people were brittle, so when they tried to make love, they simply fell apart on the ground. Coyote took pride in his creation and was not happy to see it destroyed by Sun. He called a council of the animals to determine what to do with Sun.

Coyote and the other animals met deep inside a cave away from Sun's reach and discussed what to do. All the chiefs from the great tribes of Raven, Eagle, Thunderbird and Bear came forth and spoke from their hearts. When the council finished their discussion, it was decided that Coyote would travel up into the sky and discover the reason for Sun's tyranny.

Coyote gathered up his supplies and climbed up the highest mountain. Once he reached the peak of the mountain, he jumped into the air and entered the sky.

The sky was a land just like the one he had left, except that it was bathed in a pure white light. Coyote tried to make his way to the home of Sun, but the strength of the light blinded him. He fumbled about until he came to a house. It was the house of Sun.

"Come out, great Sun spirit, and calm your light. I have traveled a long distance to deliver you this message," said Coyote.

Sun heeded Coyote's request and calmed her fury. "Why have you come here, Coyote? No man is welcome in my kingdom any longer," proclaimed Sun.

"Why? What has caused you to go into such a rage? You are normally gentle and warm, but for a long time now your fury has caused misery down on earth. Our ancient tribe can manage, but other people cannot survive. They starve when the crops do not grow and the water does not run high. You must end this fury."

"The cause of this fury is not I, Coyote," said Sun. "Long ago I was married, and every night, I would lay down with my husband, and the earth would fall into a cool darkness. But then my husband stopped coming home, and he is now in love with another. So every day I sit in my place in the sky because I have no one to lay down with."

Coyote felt sorry for Sun and offered to help her. "I will return shortly. Please calm your fury for I have someone to introduce to you."

Coyote left the home of Sun and traveled back down through the sky into his village. Calling together another council meeting, Coyote and the great chiefs of the tribes thought about how to resolve the problem of lonely Sun. But no one could come up with a solution, so Coyote took control.

"If no one shall come forth to accept this challenge, then it falls to me to solve this problem my way," said Coyote.

Coyote returned to the kingdom of the sky and transformed himself into Moon. He went to the home of Sun and proposed that they marry. Sun agreed, and they were married the next day. Moon/Coyote took his place in the sky beside his new bride and ruled the night sky.

With Moon's gentle rays shining down at night, the world was finally able to rest from the heat of the day. Life returned to the valleys and the mountains, and the ancient tribes were pleased with the work of Coyote. The Great Spirit was content, and he created the first peoples of the earth out of the fresh mud. The people prospered, and they spread through all the lands, planted their gardens and had families. All was as it should be.

Coyote, however, was troubled. After many years of pretending to be Moon, Coyote wanted to return to his old life. He looked down from above on the people and saw how much food they had to eat, the delicious salmon from the rivers and the juicy berries. After all, he was Coyote, and he did have certain desires; he also missed his long naps in the shade. Coyote could no longer keep up the deception—he changed back to his true form one night while he lay with Sun.

"Dearest Sun, please do not be upset with my deception," said Coyote. But Sun was very angry, and her fury began to burn bright once more down upon the earth. The people began to dry and break apart, and life returned to its earlier misery. The lands also became parched, there was hardly any water, and there was no relief from the heat of the day. The Great Spirit looked down upon the destruction of the world and was saddened. With that thought, the earth turned over, and everything began anew.

## Three

And there was Coyote. The Great Spirit had created the earth and placed upon it a great number of different people from countless tribes.

This was the time when the waters had disappeared. The rivers had dried up and the rains stopped falling, leaving the people in great need. The only source of water was deep underground in the roots of trees. The people tried to survive, but they began to suffer, and many of them died from lack of water.

Coyote heard the people's calls of distress and went looking for the source of the drought. For several days he walked along the dried-up riverbeds and through the parched valleys before finally entering a deep gorge that had been hollowed out between two mountains. At the base of the gorge, he noticed a small trickle of water pouring along the path that led right through and up into the mountains. Coyote followed this tiny stream that slowly began to grow in size with each step he took. He wondered if he had perhaps discovered the source of all water on earth.

He continued on up the path, following the water to its source. Coyote walked so high into the mountains that he was now above the clouds. It was a dark place where no life was present—only jagged-edged rocks spiked out of the ground. Coyote could feel the evil magic in the air and knew that someone or something was responsible for the lack of water. Despite the sense of danger, Coyote was all the more curious to find out who or what had stolen the water, and he continued along the path until he reached a large cave.

Coyote lit a torch and entered the cave, where he found a monstrous frog. Frog had been possessed by an evil spirit and was busy sucking at the source of all water on earth. He had grown to such a tremendous size that he was on the point of bursting, and despite the little trickle of water that leaked out of his eyes, the huge Frog held firm on the source of all water.

"Frog, you must release yourself from the source of water. Your gluttony knows no end. You are killing the people down in the valley," Coyote said. But Frog did not hear his words for he only knew that he had to quench his strong thirst. Nothing was going to remove him from his spot. He kept lapping up every drop he could fit into his belly; there was no end in sight to this evil.

Coyote left the cave and thought about how to extract Frog from his place over the water. Frog would not listen to reason and had no room for bargaining, so Coyote was left with only one solution.

Taking out his sharpest knife, Coyote walked up to Frog and slashed at his giant throat. He made a long gash across Frog's throat, and the skin began to rip apart as the pressure of the water forced it open. Coyote had just a few seconds to escape the cave before Frog's skin tore and a torrent of water began to pour out of the cave. The water gushed down the valley, filling up the lakes and dry riverbeds so that the people once again had fresh water. But Frog had swallowed so much water that the river burst its banks, and the water flowed into people's homes. Coyote managed to hold onto the top of the mountain while everything below was sucked under the rising waters. The great flood washed away all living things on earth, including the first peoples, who died and turned into pebbles.

After many days of water gushing forth from the cave, the torrent finally calmed and the waters returned to their normal levels. But the earth was not the same. Coyote looked down upon the land below his mountain perch and was saddened by the state of things. All the trees had been uprooted, whole mountains slid into the water and all the people created by the Great Spirit died and sank to the bottom of the great waters along the coast.

The Great Spirit saw his work destroyed and was sad. And then the earth turned over, and everything began anew.

**Four**

And there was Coyote. He wandered the earth in solitude until one day the Great Spirit created a man and a woman. They soon multiplied and spread across all the lands. These people were very clever and learned the ways of the world quickly. They lived out their lives in peace and tranquility, passing on their knowledge to future generations.

Among the people lived a young man who had fallen in the love with a beautiful woman. He tried many ways to get her to notice him, but she was not interested.

"You are too young, little one. I want a real warrior and a professional hunter as my husband. You simply tend to your parents' garden and haven't even been out on a hunt," she said, laughing at his misfortune.

This only served to anger the young man, and on that day, he vowed to become the biggest, strongest and most successful hunter of all the tribes just to prove his love to her. Every night, the young man prayed to the spirits to make him a victorious hunter and a powerful warrior, but every morning when he awoke, he was still the same young, weak man who could never win the love of the most beautiful woman he had ever seen.

Every night he prayed, but still to no avail. The young man was starting to believe that he might never become a true warrior and win the heart of the one he loved. Then one night, Coyote visited the young man.

"I have heard your calls and have come from far away to help you in your quest to win the heart of your beloved. What is it that you want from me?" asked Coyote.

"She does not see me as I am now. She wants the most powerful warrior and hunter in all of the lands. You must help me win her heart," replied the young man.

Coyote looked the young man over and saw that his heart was true. "I will give you my bow and arrow, and with it you will become the most gifted hunter in all the world. This is a bow of special design and is not to be shared with anyone. For if others were to have this knowledge, there would be great disaster," said Coyote. "To become the strongest of warriors, I will give you my arrow, but this is no ordinary arrow. It was designed in the spirit world and will make you nearly invincible. Do not give out its secret, or the world will fall into chaos. You must show respect to each animal that you slaughter and give it proper thanks for the sacrifice it made so that you may survive. This is the way of things and always has been."

Before Coyote handed over the bow and arrow, he delivered one final warning, "Be cautious, young one. If you do not return the items to me once you have won your prize, great harm will befall all people."

The young man eagerly grabbed the bow and arrow, not really heeding Coyote's warnings, and transformed into the greatest warrior in all of the lands. He immediately went into the forest and killed a deer to prove his love for the woman. When he returned to her with the deer meat and its hide, she was very impressed, but she wanted more. So the man went back into the forest and was gone for seven days. When he returned, he had killed a huge elk. Its horns were as large as tree branches, and its body was the size of 10 men. The woman was impressed with his kill but wanted still greater proof of his abilities. So the young man returned to the forest once again, and this time, he spent 14 days on the hunt. Upon his return, he presented his love with a dead bear. But still she was not satisfied, and the young man continued to stalk the forest for the biggest beasts to bring home to his love. Every morning before sunrise, he left on the hunt, stalked the woods and delivered a sure death to any animal that came within his sights.

After the young man proved his strength as a hunter to the woman, she finally accepted his advances and they were soon married. But the weapons Coyote had given him had changed the young man; he had come to enjoy the thrill of the kill and hunted out of want and not need.

The couple had many sons, and when they had grown up, they too began to seek out wives. The sons came to their father and asked him to reveal his hunting secrets. They begged their father until he finally showed them the bow and arrow that Coyote had bestowed upon him so many years ago. The sons copied the weapons and became great hunters and spread across the lands in search of the most beautiful wives. Although they became successful hunters, the people forgot to pay their respects to the animals for their sacrifice. As the generations passed on the knowledge of how to make the weapons, more and more great hunters emerged. Soon every tribe had become very efficient in the hunt, and people began hunting more animals than they needed.

The big animals were the first to disappear; there were no more buffalo in the valleys, no more elk grazing in the forests, and even the powerful bear, strongest of the animal tribes, fell under the arrows of the people. When the large animals were gone, the people hunted beaver, mink and even squirrel, until they, too, disappeared.

Then the people moved to the waters and excelled in the hunt there, too. The people devoured all the salmon in the rivers, the trout in the lakes and the halibut in the seas. Farther and farther the hunters pushed into the wilderness with the skill of the bow and arrow leading their path. When the deep forests were cleared of animals, the people climbed to the very tops of mountains and swam to the deepest part of the earth in the thrill of the hunt.

The people were so successful at hunting that after many generations, the earth fell silent. Only the sound of the people could be heard. The Great Spirit wept when he saw what had become of his creation.

Coyote had warned the people not to take more than they needed with the bow and arrow, but the excitement of the hunt had become part of the people's essence, and they no longer respected the spirit world. As their punishment, the Great Spirit turned the people into the animals of the world. They became beaver, eagle, buffalo, bear and deer. And then the earth turned over, and everything began again.

And always there was Coyote.

We now live in the age of the fifth creation. We must pay homage to the spirits and respect all that is around us. If not, the world will turn over, and everything will begin anew.

# The Great Reformation

LONG AGO, BEFORE THE MEMORY of all humans, the Great Spirit called all the animal people together. The Great Spirit told them that he was happy with their work on earth but that it was time for the world to change. "There will be a new kind of people in this world soon, and they will spread far and wide across this earth.

"I have decided that you will all receive new names. I know some of you, like Coyote and Bear, already have names, but some of you don't. At first light tomorrow, you will all return to my lodge and you will be able to choose your new names. The first person through the door will get first choice of names, the second person will get second choice, and so on and so on, until no names remain," the Great Spirit told the animal people.

After listening to what the Great Spirit had told them, all the animals talked among themselves about which names they would like to take. Each animal wanted the most powerful and respected of names and vowed to be the first in line the following day. Coyote was the most vocal of the animals, boasting that he would be first in line to take the most respected name. He had lived with his name too long and wanted a new one. The name "Coyote" had become synonymous with trickery and foolishness. He was the great imitator, and no one wanted to hold his name.

"I will be the first and choose a new name, and then someone else will know the stigma of holding the name of Coyote," he said. "I will choose the name of Grizzly Bear and become the most powerful animal to walk on land, or I shall choose the name of Eagle and rule the skies, or I will become Sea Wolf and become master of the water tribes."

"But, dear Brother," said Fox. "No one wants your name, and everyone will fight to be first in line to choose, just like you."

"When I am the all-powerful Grizzly Bear, I will show all the people how it feels to be deemed shiftless and sneaky, as I am treated now," boasted Coyote.

"Whatever name you want to choose is not yet yours, so you better get some rest and be awake at first light, or you will remain forever with the name Coyote," warned Fox.

This was wise advice from Fox, but Coyote did not pay any attention to his brother's words because he was too involved in his own importance. "I will stay up all night so as not to be the last of the animals to choose a name. I will be the greatest animal in all the world, and all will be forced to recognize my power."

Coyote returned to his home and continued to dream of his new name. "Tomorrow I will become someone important, someone respected, someone whose name will forever be remembered in the annals of our history. I will do great things with my new name. I think I will become Grizzly Bear and devour my enemies in one bite," he said to himself, then he thought, "No, maybe I will become Eagle, so I can soar above the world as free as the wind. The choice will be hard to make, so I will stay awake all night and think over my decision."

Coyote gathered a load of firewood to last the night and sat down to think over his new name. He was full of energy at the start of the evening, but as the night wore on and the fire warmed him, he became tired and his eyes began to close.

Before long, Coyote fell asleep, and when he awoke, the sun was already high in the sky.

Rushing down to the lodge of the Great Spirit, Coyote burst through the door and found no other animal there waiting. "Could it be that I am first?" he thought. Walking up to Great Spirit, Coyote announced, "Since I am the first, I will take the name of the great Grizzly Bear."

"The name you have chosen was selected at sunrise and cannot be taken again," said the Great Spirit.

"Then I will take the name of Eagle and fly free in the sky," proclaimed Coyote.

"The owner of that name flew off bright and early this morning," said Great Spirit.

Now a little worried, Coyote then blurted out his third choice, "Then if it must be, I will take the name of Sea Wolf."

"You are too late for that name as well; it took to the waters two hours ago," said Great Spirit.

Coyote's pride-filled heart suddenly sank with sadness. All the names had already been taken, even Mosquito and Tick—only the name Coyote was left.

"Do not despair, noble Coyote, for it was my will that you missed all the great names. I have saved a special distinction for you. You will become the chief of all the tribes and protector of the new people that are to come," said Great Spirit. "Across these lands there are many beasts and monsters that terrorize and kill the people so that they do not prosper, remaining weak and scared. It is to you that I give magical powers to defeat the beasts and teach the people the ways of the world. With this power you can change into anything you can think of and do all kinds of magical things that you never imagined. You might have missed out on being Grizzly Bear, but there is no shame in the task to which you have been assigned."

Coyote left the lodge of the Great Spirit with a renewed confidence. He had become a chief after all! Walking among the people, Coyote boasted of the powers bestowed upon him by the Great Spirit and how important he would be to the new people on earth. However, nothing had changed in Coyote—he was still the same prideful creature they had known earlier, and the people continued to ignore him. But to Coyote himself, he was the chief of all peoples, the most powerful among them.

# Order and Chaos

**Part One: Order**

LONG AGO, BEFORE OUR grandfather's grandfather walked this world, the earth was much different than it is at present. There were no trees and no grasslands; neither were there any salmon or berries to eat. The people who lived during this age were called speta'kl. They were animals, but not like we know them today, for although they had the appearance of the beasts of the world, parts of them took on a human form.

The speta'kl lived a life on this earth that was short, nasty and brutish. Since there was so little to offer the people for food and shelter, fighting was commonplace, and out in the shadow lands, there remained the ever-present danger of the cannibal tribes. But the good people of the earth were bestowed with magical powers by the Great Spirit, and they set about making the world a better place to live. But the task was not easy.

One of the most powerful creatures of the speta'kl was known as Coyote, and although he was a sly character, his intentions were always good, and he aimed to please the Great Spirit.

Coyote lived in a village with Wolf, Owl, Eagle and Bear. As Coyote was the most powerful of them all, he was named the chief. Tired of living in fear of the world outside their village and going without proper food and water, the members of the clan were called to council, and it was decided that Coyote would leave the village and travel the forbidden lands to do battle with the forces that sought to destroy all the good in the world.

"The Great Spirit has created us for this task," Coyote told the council. "Seeing as I am the most powerful creature among us, I will leave the village and travel great distances to turn chaos into order."

"But there are dangers out in the land of shadows that not even your magic can defeat. These beasts are of such size and power that even the Great Spirit trembles," replied wise Owl.

"Quiet your worries, Owl," said Eagle. "Do not disparage our chief and the Great Spirit, for though this quest is fraught with danger, Coyote will have our help when he needs it, as well as the guidance of the Great Spirit himself."

"You humble me, Eagle, with your words," said Coyote. "At first light tomorrow, I will leave on my journey and not return until I have made this world a peaceful place."

**Part Two: Chaos**

Early the next morning, Coyote packed a light bag and headed out along the path toward the forbidden lands where monsters and demons dwelled. For many days, Coyote traveled the path, not once encountering another soul. Weary from the journey, Coyote stepped off the path to catch his breath. It was then that he spotted a small village through the haze of the sun. Blinded by the sun and tired from traveling, Coyote decided to stop and ask the people of the village for a drink of water. Expecting to see people outside their homes going about their daily lives, Coyote was surprised when no one came out to greet him. In fact, the only sign of life was a plume of smoke rising from the chimney of one of the homes. Upon entering the house, Coyote could barely make out the shapes of several people sitting beside a fire. Not one of the people moved as Coyote entered the room, for all their attention was focused on a boiling birchbark sack.

"Excuse me, kind people of this land!" shouted Coyote to get their attention.

An elderly man slowly turned his head to see who had spoken. Coyote could see that the old man's eyes were clouded over with white, and the few remaining teeth in his mouth were blackened and about to fall out.

"What is it you want, stranger?" scolded the old man, upset at being interrupted.

"I have come to ask your assistance. I have been traveling for days. I am in need of water and perhaps something to eat," said Coyote.

All at once, the people gathered around the fire began to laugh in the most sinister fashion. Now able to see the faces of the other people sitting around the fire, Coyote was suddenly afraid. The people had bald patches on their heads and, like the old man, most of their teeth had rotted and fallen out. Coyote could not help but wonder what ill fate had befallen them.

"You ask for food, stranger, when we have not had a meal in days," said the old man. "Look at our pot. It is filled with the most bitter roots and rancid meat. We salivate over this like dogs while the monster eats his fill."

"For as long as we can remember, the monster has diverted our waters, stolen our fish and destroyed our crops," said one emaciated villager. "We survive on the bones it discards and bitter roots. Once we were a proud people, but when the monster came, he took everything."

"I have not seen any monsters," said Coyote.

"You will," replied the old man.

"Nonsense, good people. I am the all-powerful Coyote, and I have come to restore life to your lands. Give me time, and you shall see your lands prosper," promised Coyote. With that, he left the little house and immediately set to work.

Coyote could see that the village's great river (today called the Columbia) had been picked up and moved so that it now flowed down from the mountains. Using his magic, Coyote lifted the great river and placed it in its original spot. Seeing this great miracle brought a sense of hope back to the people of the village, but they knew it would not be long before the great beast would come to reclaim his prize. As Coyote finished his work of repositioning the river, a noise thundered in the distance.

"It is here," sobbed the old man.

After getting the people to safety, Coyote hid behind a rock and waited for the mythical monster to show itself. A terror like he had never felt before gripped Coyote as he stared out into the mountain range waiting for the beast to emerge. Suddenly,

Coyote saw a great head appear in the distance. Never before had he witnessed such a sight—way off somewhere melting into the horizon, Coyote could just make out a gigantic body. As it came over the top of the mountain, the monster's body blocked out the sun and cast an ominous shadow over the entire village.

Even from a distance, Coyote could see that it was not going to be easy to defeat the beast. Its poisonous fangs hung outside its huge mouth, and the monster's saliva fell to the ground, eating away at the soil. One of its gigantic claws was the size of Coyote, and with each step, the monster dug deep into the ground, causing the earth to tremble. This was a creature like no other, and to stop it, Coyote would have to call upon all his powers.

"Halt, beast!" yelled out Coyote. "You do not belong here! Leave this world in peace, or I shall be forced to kill you!"

Looking around with his giant head, the monster spotted Coyote standing defiantly before him. Seeing the little figure standing in his path, the monster let out a deep laugh. "Foolish being. You are so small. Get out of my way and let me reclaim what is mine, little fool, or you shall be swallowed like so many others that have gotten in my way."

It was then that Coyote realized how he would be able to defeat the beast. "Go ahead and swallow me whole, monster," taunted Coyote. "I am Coyote, and I cannot be defeated!"

The monster simply laughed and inhaled Coyote into his mouth with one big gulp. On his way down the throat of the beast, Coyote noticed the remains of many people who had failed to make it out alive. When he entered the monster's stomach, he came across two boys.

"How did you end up here?" asked Coyote.

"We were simply looking for a drink when we were sucked into a great black hole and ended up here," said one of the boys.

"If you show me the way to the heart, I will get you out of here," said Coyote.

The boys agreed and led Coyote through the monster's veins directly to the chamber that held the heart. Taking out his knife, Coyote cut the arteries connected to the monster's massive heart. The monster began to writhe in pain, but all went suddenly silent once Coyote cut the last artery. The beast was dead. Coyote and the boys then walked back out of the monster's mouth and into the sunshine. Coyote removed the bones of the beast and created the great trees of the coast that remain to this day.

Returning to the village, Coyote spoke with the people. "Hear this, good people of the village. You no longer have to worry about the great beast that plagued your village. The river has been returned to its rightful place, and the salmon will soon follow. Rejoice, for Coyote has brought you back to life."

A great cheer went up from the people of the village, and they spent several days in celebration. Coyote then packed a few supplies and some water and headed back out on his quest. For days he traveled west until he came to a land where few ventured. He had arrived in the land of shadows where dwelt a tribe of cannibals.

Coyote had heard many tales of these people—how they devoured the flesh of their own kind down to the bone—but he had never believed people capable of such horrors. Yet as he walked along the path leading to their camp, he began to feel the presence of a great evil in the air.

The air became clouded with acrid, black smoke. The earth itself was not brown but was scarred black from fire and littered with the bones of thousands upon thousands of the cannibals' victims. Coyote thought to himself that this truly was a land that had been forgotten by the Great Spirit. The path before his feet began to disappear in the dense air, and soon Coyote could barely see in front of him.

Despite every part of his being telling him to leave this cursed landscape, Coyote kept moving forward. It was his goal to put the world in order and, therefore, no obstacle would block his path. But Coyote was no fool, and the tribe of cannibals was a dangerous bunch that could not be approached easily.

Coyote paused along the path, sitting on a rock to ease his tired feet. As he was pondering his next move, he saw something charge toward him through the hazy, smoke-filled air. Coyote retrieved his knife and held it in front of him for fear he might be someone's next meal. Using his keen sense of hearing, Coyote was able to hear the rapid breathing of someone in distress. Lowering his knife, he whispered into the black haze, "Over here. It is safe. I am a friend."

Bursting through the smoke came Salamander with a look of abject horror frozen on his face. Coyote looked down at Salamander's body and saw that one of his legs had been eaten off.

"You have to help me," pleaded Salamander. "Those animals are right behind me and are looking to finish off what they started."

"Fear not, my friend, for I will help you. I am the all-powerful Coyote, slayer of giant beasts," boasted Coyote. "What has happened to you?"

"I was taking in some sun along the edge of a river when I was knocked over the head. When I awoke, I was in the most horrible of places. I was tied down to a table, and I could not move any of my limbs. That was when I saw them. Eyes of pure white stared back at me from all corners of the dark room. I could hear them muttering to one another, but I could not make sense of their garbled noises. Several of them stood over me, and through the faint light I could see that I had been captured by the cannibals. They did not have faces like you or I. Their noses were simply two holes in their faces, and their skin was covered in boils and was of a rotting greenish brown color. I can hardly close my eyes lest I see their faces again. But the worst part was their teeth—hundreds of razor-sharp teeth in rows that could tear the hide off any beast. They stood about me, barely able to keep the drool in their mouths, and then all of them descended on my leg, eating my flesh as I watched. Once they had devoured every part of my leg including the bone, they retired from the room, leaving me bound, with the obvious intention of returning to finish off their meal. But in their eating frenzy, they had loosened my ties, and I managed to escape."

Coyote listened to the tale of Salamander without uttering a single word. When Salamander had finished telling his terrible tale, Coyote finally spoke. "For your great suffering, I will give you something that will serve you and your kind for all eternity."

Coyote then took a magical herb and spread it over Salamander's hip where his leg used to be, and, in an instant, Salamander's leg grew back.

"This is a gift I give to you and your kind. If ever you are caught and lose one of your limbs, it will grow back just as good as new," said Coyote. "Now run from this place. I have come up with a way to deal with these infernal beasts."

After thanking Coyote several times, Salamander ran off and disappeared from sight. Once Salamander was safely out of harm's way, Coyote immediately set about putting his plan into action. Instead of confronting the cannibals in a show of force, Coyote decided to use his substantial powers of intellect.

He took another magical herb from his sack and sprinkled some of the powder on a rock. In the blink of an eye, the rock turned into the lifeless body of a beautiful woman. But this was no ordinary body, for Coyote had used a special magic to transform the body into something so much more.

Coyote dragged the beautiful woman's body close to the village where the cannibals had gathered. He found that most of them were hurriedly moving about the village, frantically searching for their escaped prisoner. Placing the body where he was sure the cannibals would find it, Coyote hid from sight and waited for his plan to unfold.

He watched patiently for several minutes, and then one of the tribe, a stubby character with drooling fangs, happened upon the body and immediately let out a lustful grunt that alerted the rest of the beasts. Coyote watched in horror as the horde of cannibals descended on the body and tore it to pieces. They ripped off limbs, tore at the dead woman's gut and lingered on her neck, savoring every morsel of flesh until every last piece had been consumed. Coyote was almost sick at the sight of such depravity. As the beasts sat back and licked bits of flesh from their claws, Coyote came out from his hiding spot and announced his presence.

"Foul creatures," pronounced Coyote. "Your time has come to an end. No longer will you feast on other beings. I have come to put an end to your miserable existence."

The cannibals snarled at Coyote, gnashing their teeth and licking their disfigured lips with the prospect of yet another easy meal. But when they tried to get up, they found that they were held fast in place.

"The body you just tore apart was not the flesh of a young, beautiful woman but my own work of magic. In your haste to feed your appetites, you have forgotten the humanity bestowed upon you by the Great Spirit. The savagery in which you have so lustfully partaken has warped your figures, sharpened your teeth and left your minds dull and stupid," said Coyote scornfully. "What you just ate will now take the last morsels of humanity left in you and turn turn you into what you truly are."

With a wave of Coyote's hand and a bright flash, the tribe of cannibals changed into mosquitoes. "You are now a pestilence to the rest of the world. Your existence will be one of suffering, hatred and disease. Your bite will forever just be an annoyance to the world and will make you the most hated creature on the planet."

Having defeated the cannibals, Coyote used his magic to bring their dead land back to life. Simply by using his thoughts, Coyote returned the trees to the soil, brought back the rivers and the lakes and seeded the expansive valleys with life. Once his work was completed, Coyote returned to the path and continued on his journey.

## Part Three: Chaos

Coyote put his ear to the wind and heard the faint whisper of a breeze pass by. It was a sign to go west, toward the waters, into the setting sun. For days, Coyote passed through the valleys, traversed mountains and crossed lakes before coming to a stop at a very peculiar place.

It was a small village high in the mountains, but it was like no village he had ever seen before. The people did not live in houses like the ones he had come across in the Okanogan Valley. They had actually buried their homes inside the mountain. In front of each entrance hole, they had placed a large stone door that Bear would have had trouble moving. Coyote called out to the people, but no answer came back. Looking up at the top of the mountain, Coyote could see a great deal of smoke coming from its peak, and he noticed the smell of salmon in the air. He knew people still inhabited this land.

He tried knocking on one of the doors, and after a minute, the stone door creaked to life and began to open. From the darkness of the cave emerged a large pair of eyes that were filled with terror.

"We have not seen a traveler through our lands in a long time," trembled the voice belonging to those terrified eyes. "Why are you not affffraid, strangerrr?"

"I do not see anything to fear here," replied Coyote with confidence. "I am Coyote—surely you have heard of me. Now why should I be afraid?"

"Please enter. Quickly!" said the voice. "And I will relate to you our great misfortunes."

Coyote followed the voice down a long, black tunnel into the main chamber of the home. In the center of the room a fire burned, and gathered around was an entire family. The eldest of the family stood up and spoke first.

"Please, join us," said the old man, pointing to a spot next to the fire, where a small piece of salmon was slowly cooking. "You may share our meager portion of salmon even though it is all we have eaten in a long time. We are a people living under the tyranny of Thunderbird."

With the mention of the name, everyone in the group suddenly shuddered with fear. "We have built these homes into the mountain because it is the only place we are safe from its wrath," continued the old man.

"Who is this Thunderbird?" asked Coyote.

"For as long as we can remember, our tribe has lived in this valley, fishing salmon out of the rivers and farming the rich soil that stretches to the coast. But we are continually forced to pay dues to Thunderbird. He lives high up in the mountains, and from his perch he watches us. If we do not please him, he terrorizes us by batting his wings to create strong winds, and he batters us down with booming thunder and shoots lightning bolts from his eyes when he does not get his wish. Even when we have met his demands, he still unleashes his anger upon us."

"All he leaves us is the scraps from his dinner," added a young mother who held a crying infant at her breast.

The plight of these hard-working people saddened Coyote, and he decided to return order to the chaos. After sitting with the people and hearing more stories of tyranny and oppression from above, Coyote tried to sleep that night, but outside the stone doors, Thunderbird raged; he beat his wings and flashed his lightning in anger over the visitor. The force of the wind tossed rocks all about, the thunder banged so loud that it nearly knocked the air from the people's lungs, and the lightning flashed brighter than the midday sun. Coyote knew that Thunderbird was as old as time and therefore very wise. But Coyote was more powerful and possessed a wisdom second only to that of the Great Spirit.

In the morning, Coyote awoke to an eerie calm. Not a sound could be heard outside, for all life had taken shelter from the fury of the Thunderbird. No one dared move lest they upset him again. Coyote had fought under such impossible odds before, but this situation was different; he was facing a power much like his own—a power that had been in existence as long as his own and that could not be extinguished by pure force. Coyote sat inside the cave and thought out his plan for several days while Thunderbird continued to rage, calling for offerings.

Finally, Coyote could think up no better plan than simply walking up to Thunderbird and talking to him. If Coyote's words could reach Thunderbird's ears through the thunder of his wings, then maybe he might calm his fury. Taking his sack along with him, Coyote took the path up the mountain. In front of him lay an arduous trail edged with steep cliffs, and up in the clouds awaited one of Coyote's greatest challenges.

High above the village, beyond the reach of the clouds, Thunderbird sat and watched Coyote making his way up the path.

"What punishments must I think of for these people for sending someone to disrupt the almighty Thunderbird?" the ancient spirit bellowed down the mountainside as he caught sight of Coyote in the distance. He began flapping his wings, whipping up violent winds and knocking Coyote to the ground, nearly sending him flying off the edge of the cliff. But Coyote held fast and continued to push his way up the path.

"Foolish Thunderbird, it is Coyote. Surely you remember your ancient cousin, we of the first ones to walk this earth. Calm your fury and let the people live in peace."

"I know you, Coyote of the first tribes. But there is nothing you can do or say that will put an end to my anger. This is not your business. Now be gone!" screeched Thunderbird, releasing lightning from his big eyes and pounding his chest so hard that the noise cracked just above Coyote's head.

It was a frightful display, but Coyote held firm and pushed forward. Thunderbird had created such a disturbance that he woke the clouds from their home high in the mountains and out poured a torrential rain and hailstorm upon Coyote. But Coyote pressed on through the deluge and called out to Thunderbird, "Though your anger be great, all your efforts are in vain."

Coyote continued up the path and, before long, he broke through the clouds and walked into the home of Thunderbird. At the edge of the mountain perch stood the great creature, whose great size nearly blocked out the sun. For the moment, Thunderbird calmed his fury, folded his wings and stared down upon Coyote with his all-seeing eyes.

"What do you want, ancient one?" demanded Thunderbird.

"The people that live in the valley below talk of suffering and living under tyranny. Does your anger against these people never end?" asked Coyote.

"This is none of your business, Coyote. You have entered my world, where I am the most powerful. The people below have continually failed me and must be punished," bellowed Thunderbird.

"What is it they have done?" asked Coyote.

"They do not pay proper respect to the spirits of this world. They take what they don't need and waste what the Great Spirit has given them," replied Thunderbird. "And long ago, one of their tribe members was sent up to my mountain perch, and he tried to slay me. I have been on this earth too long to take such disrespect with good humor, Coyote. I have been punishing the foolish tribe for many years and shall continue throughout time as long as the people do not show respect."

"I found the people down below to have grown and matured over the years, and the ones you said had shown great disrespect are no longer on this earth. They have mended their ways for the better," pleaded Coyote.

"This I do not believe," replied Thunderbird.

"While they will never be perfect, I have a solution that will solve everything. I cannot return to the people without an answer, as I, too, am a powerful spirit with a reputation to uphold, so let us compromise," bargained Coyote. "The people will always need a reminder when they do not pay respect to the spirits. Whenever you see any bad behavior, it is left to you to flash your lightning, thunder your wings and stir up the clouds. This will let the people know that they have angered Thunderbird."

"You have more faith in these creatures than I do, Coyote. But I will do as you request and only unleash my anger upon them when they forget the traditions," said Thunderbird.

"I thank you, noble spirit," said Coyote as he returned to the path.

From that day forth, whenever the skies thundered and lightning flashed, it meant that someone had failed to remember to pay respect to the spirits and had unleashed the anger of the great Thunderbird.

## Part Four: Order

Coyote returned to his travels. After he had journeyed for many days, he heard a sound coming the north. With each step, the noise got louder and louder—at first it was just a faint whisper, but soon it grew into a full concert of what sounded like the moans and wails of people in torment.

Approaching the source of the noise, Coyote stumbled upon the most unfortunate of scenes.

He happened upon a village whose inhabitants were gathered outside, weeping over the spirits of dead family members. There were at least 50 people gathered in the center of the village, and they were all kneeling on the ground facing north. They screamed out loud, tore at their skin and pulled at their hair in grief over a lost lover or family member. Coyote had walked into a village plagued by grief.

Mourning songs could be heard from the mouths of each person as they told of their suffering and overwhelming sorrow. The display of emotion confused Coyote because it is said that everything dies and then travels to the land of the dead, but these people seemed to have forgotten the way of things and were in anguish over the loss of their loved ones.

Coyote approached the eldest of the villagers and asked, "Why do you sing songs of death and pain? Do you not know the way of things?"

But the eldest was blinded by his grief. "Do not speak to me of natural order, traveler! All my life I had tried for a son, and after having 10 daughters, the Great Spirit blessed me with one son. But he was taken away from me and now sits in the land of the dead. How can this be? When leaves turn brown and die with the coming of autumn, and the trees stand bare and cold, I can see after the snows have departed that spring brings the leaves back to the trees and the verdure returns to the forests. Then why does my son not return?" the old man pleaded. "I harvest my crops, and again they return to life the next season and continue to nourish my people for generations. Why must my son stay in the land of the dead?"

The old man did not wait for Coyote to answer; he was overcome once again with grief and began to beat his temples and cry to the heavens. The people's suffering filled Coyote with sorrow, and he meditated for several days on how he might bring this man's son and everyone else's loved ones back to the land of the living. For although Coyote was a powerful being, he, too, had grieved for loved ones. He knew the task to be nearly impossible, but Coyote's heart had opened to the suffering of the people.

"As the rebirth of life comes every spring, I will go to the land of the dead and restore your loved ones to this world," pronounced Coyote to the village. "I will meditate for three days, and when I emerge, I will have a way of getting your families back, for I am Coyote."

Retreating to a quiet part of the forest, Coyote sat in a small clearing underneath a mighty tree and meditated on his task. When he came out of the forest on the fourth day, Coyote traveled to the home of Eagle. Coyote remembered that Eagle had lost his wife and son and was still in mourning for their passing. He would be more than willing to accompany Coyote on the long journey.

"Besides, the land of the dead is far away, and I don't want to walk," thought Coyote.

Once Eagle heard the plan to go to the land of the dead and return all the lost souls back to the living, he immediately packed some supplies, threw Coyote on his back and took to the sky. High into the air they soared over deep river valleys, over jagged mountaintops and off to the ends of the earth, where they came to a great expanse of water.

In the distance, shrouded in fog, Coyote spotted an island populated with many houses, but not a soul could be seen. Eagle called out to the island, but no answer came back.

"Come, Coyote, get on my back, and I will fly us over the water," said Eagle.

"We have arrived when the sun is high. The dead only come out when the moon shines at night. We must wait patiently by the shore. Passage to and from the island is by boat only. It is the ferry for the dead," replied Coyote.

Coyote and Eagle waited patiently along the shore for a few days, occasionally fishing for a meal and sleeping in the shade, until dusk one evening when the moon appeared bright overhead.

Eagle called out, "People of the island, we need safe passage to your island."

A light illuminated on the distant shore, and Eagle and Coyote watched as two dark figures in a boat began to paddle out toward them. As the boat approached, they saw that its bottom did not even touch the water. It simply floated above the still water and glided to a halt in front of Coyote and Eagle.

Without a word, the men on the boat beckoned them to board. Looking at the faces of the men from up close, Coyote saw that their eyes were open but completely blackened, and their mouths had been sewn shut.

As they neared the shore of the island, the sounds of singing, drumming and dancing could be heard from across the water. After they landed, the two travelers were left on the beach alone, and they watched as the boat disappeared into the darkness.

"I hope they come back," remarked Eagle.

Following the sounds of the music and dancing, Coyote and Eagle came upon a sight they had not expected. Entering the largest house on the island, they were amazed at the beauty of what lay before them. The house was adorned with elaborate mats, and all the people were dressed in the most noble fashion. They danced about in the light of the moon, and all looked very content. Coyote could not believe what he was witnessing. He had fully expected to find the same amount of grief as he had left behind in the village, but instead, the people here laughed with one another, danced and had a plentiful banquet for their taking.

Eagle gazed about the room looking for a familiar face. His eyes suddenly stopped on two faces—those of his wife and son. Eagle called out their names, but they could neither see nor hear him. No matter what Eagle did, he could not get his beloved to look him in the eye. Coyote saw some of his dead relatives and also could not get them to acknowledge his presence; it was as if he was a ghost.

Angered by the rejection, Eagle removed a small box from his bundle and explained to Coyote that it could be used to capture all the people. "Once they are inside the box, only then will we be able to get back to the land of the living with all our loved ones," said Eagle.

"This cannot be, Eagle," replied Coyote. "This is a sacred place. The people are happy here. Look how they dance about. It is our grief that we wish to alleviate, not theirs. To take them would be against the will of the Great Spirit."

But Eagle would not listen. The grief for his family was just too much for him to bear, and when he opened up the box, all the people in the land of the dead were trapped inside. Eagle flew out of the house with his box to the beach where the boatmen had left their canoe. Coyote ran after Eagle and pleaded for him to return, but Eagle stole the canoe and paddled back to the land of the living. But once he arrived, all was not as it should have been.

Upon opening the box, all the souls of the dead appeared, but they did not sing, they did not dance, and they did not seem content. Their faces had lost all color and had turned blue. Their lips were chalk white, and the life in their eyes that had once been was now gone. Soon the people began to mourn the return of their loved ones as they saw how much pain they were in.

It was then that the Great Spirit appeared before Eagle in the form of an old man. He took the box from Eagle and gathered all the people inside with just a thought. "Eagle, your love for your family is great, but it has led you to upset the way of things. Things are born, and then they die. It has been that way ever since I willed it so and shall never change until a time of my choosing. You will come back with me and return the universe to order," said the old man.

Once he was in the land of the dead, Eagle opened the box and released the souls back to their homes. Coyote returned to the shores and watched as the dead drifted through their doorways and the music and dancing started up once more.

"All is as it should be," spoke the Great Spirit. "Coyote, your work is done on this earth for now. You will return with me to the land in the heavens, and you will be called upon when you are needed. Death is life continued, and you cannot return from that path once you have started the journey."

With that, the Great Spirit returned everything to how it once was, and the people were happy for they had seen how the dead suffered in the land of the living. Knowing their loved ones were content, the people of the grief-stricken village continued on with their lives and, although they still wept for the passing of their loved ones, they now did so with joy.

# Fire

WE LOOK UPON FIRE AS a mere tool, but in the time long ago, our people did not have fire. When the sun went down, there was no fire for comfort, and when the hunt was successful, there was no fire to cook the meat. The people were in great need of fire, and seeing his people suffer greatly disturbed Coyote. It was then that he decided that something must be done. There was fire in the sky—all one had to do was to retrieve it from the source.

The first problem was that the sky was too far for Coyote to reach. So he took out his arrow, aimed it toward the sky and let the bolt fly high up into the air. The arrow traveled for some distance until it came to a halt when it pierced the sky. Coyote then took all the arrows in his possession and began firing them into the sky. One by one they landed, hitting each other in a straight line so that when Coyote finally ran out of arrows, he had constructed a "rope" all the way into the heavens.

After packing a few supplies, Coyote began his climb up the rope into the sky. He pulled himself up past the trees, over the mountains and through the clouds before finally reaching the end. Coyote then took out his knife and carved a hole in the sky. Crawling through the opening, he came out into a place that he could not have imagined. Before him was a world much like the one he had just left, but it was much more peaceful and beautiful. The rivers were teeming with salmon, the forests were in full bloom and the people walked about happy and content. Coyote found this to be a very special place and was more than willing to sample its delights. For days, Coyote walked among the people of the sky and was treated to the greatest hospitality. He was fed the fattest salmon, dined on the juiciest berries and was given the most comfortable of beds on which to rest. What started out as a few days gradually turned into weeks, and all the while, the people back on earth suffered in cold misery.

Soon the people on earth began to wonder if Coyote had been captured or perhaps killed on his quest for fire, so it was left to his brother Fox to follow Coyote's path up the rope and into the world of the sky to find out what had happened. Fox climbed up the rope, up over the trees, over the mountains, through the clouds and into the hole Coyote had cut open in the sky. Fox was amazed by the landscape that opened before his eyes and knew this land would have the power to hold Coyote there.

Fox searched and searched until he finally found Coyote asleep in the grass by the edge of a river. He was surrounded by the bones of many salmon and had obviously fallen asleep after eating his fill. Fox yelled at him to wake up. "Come, Coyote, we must return to earth with fire or else the people face grave times. We need not lose any more of our brothers and sisters to the cold when the solution is so close at hand. WAKE UP!"

Coyote sat up straight from his slumber and looked at Fox. "Come and join me, Brother, this place is wonderful," he said. "You will forget all the troubles of the world you have left."

But Fox remained insistent and pulled Coyote from his gluttonous slumber. Together, the two traveled to the largest house in the entire world in the sky where the fire was held. It was a sacred place that was guarded by some of the sky people's most fearsome warriors. Four warriors stood outside the house's door at all times and watched for days on end. Coyote and Fox spent several days just watching the house from the cover of the forest before finally coming up with an idea to steal the fire.

While observing the house, they had noticed that none of the warriors had anything to eat or drink during their long hours of standing guard over the home. Coyote knew that no man could resist a full meal when his stomach ached, and he decided to use this as a means of distracting the guards and slipping into the house. So Coyote transformed some rocks into the most decadent of meals for the warriors and placed it in front of them. Without hesitation, all four men planted their faces in their food and took their eyes and minds off the house. Fox and Coyote took the opportunity to sneak inside the doorway and into the inner chamber that held the fire.

They entered a large cavernous room where at the far end a great ball of fire floated freely in the air above the ground. Its light filled every corner of the room, casting no shadows, but it did not blind either Coyote or Fox for its glow was soft and warm. Coyote then took a stick out of his sack and stuck it into the great ball of light. Instantly, the end of the stick ignited, and Coyote held it aloft in triumph. Coyote and Fox quickly left the great room, but when they opened the door to the outside, they found that the guards had finished their meal and were searching for the intruders.

Coyote and Fox ran at full speed toward the hole they had cut into the sky. But in their haste, as Fox was running in front of Coyote, he tripped, causing Coyote to fall forward onto Fox's tail with the burning flame. Fox managed to blow it out, but the accident left Fox with a permanent mark on his tail that can still be seen today.

Luckily, Coyote and Fox managed to reach the hole in the sky and escape the clutches of their pursuers. After traveling down the rope of arrows, Coyote and Fox gathered all the people together to present them with the gift of fire. Seeing the dancing flame, many tried to touch it and quickly learned of its power. Coyote gave each of the chiefs part of the flame that came from the people of the sky. Now the people could cook their food and keep themselves warm in winter.

# Curiosity and the Blackbird

COYOTE WAS WALKING OVER THE mountains and through the forests one day when the sky suddenly turned as black as night. He looked up toward a nearby mountain and could see that the spirit Thunderbird had been angered. The winds began to pick up from the flapping of his wings, thunder sounded overhead and lightning bolts shot through the sky. Coyote did not like to be outside when the weather raged, and he began searching for cover.

He entered a dark forest hoping to find some shelter among the giant trees. Through the wind and the rain, Coyote spotted a gigantic cedar tree that was hollow.

But the entryway of the tree was too small for Coyote to get through, so he called out, "Open, tree. I am Coyote, and you must let me in from the storm."

To his amazement, an entrance appeared and allowed Coyote inside. He then called out, "Close, tree. I, Coyote, am inside." The tree closed its bark and sealed Coyote inside, protecting him from the raging storm.

Coyote lay down on the soft ground. He expected a long wait because anytime Thunderbird worked himself into a rage, it could last for hours or even days. Coyote waited inside the tree for two days before Thunderbird finally calmed his fury. Wanting to get outside and ease his hungry stomach, Coyote called out to the tree again. "Open, tree. I am Coyote, and I want to get out."

But the tree did not move. Coyote tried speaking to the tree again, this time using a softer voice, "Please, dear tree. I wish to exit your hollow trunk so that I might go eat my fill." But again the tree did not open. Coyote flew into a rage, kicking and clawing at the inside of the tree, but still the tree did not open.

After calming down, Coyote began to think. After some contemplation, Coyote remembered that he was the chief of all animals and called out for the help of the forest creatures to free him from his wooden prison.

First, he called out to the birds to peck a hole into the bark big enough for him to get through. The first to try was Goose. He pecked and pecked at the rock-solid wood and only ended up wearing down his bill until it was flat and round. Coyote then called to Sparrow, but his beak was too small and did not even make a mark on the tough bark of the giant cedar tree. Coyote needed a bird with a stronger beak and called forth Owl, Raven and Eagle to help him escape. But the three birds could do little more than chip away at the tough bark, leaving only a small, smooth patch.

Coyote was becoming impatient. Finally, he called upon Woodpecker to help him out. Woodpecker hammered away at the wood with his powerful beak and managed to pierce through the cedar. But the hole was barely big enough to fit Woodpecker, and Coyote was much larger than the little bird.

Coyote began to pace about in the hollow tree trying to think of a way out. The birds had nearly worn off their beaks trying to extract him from the clutches of the cedar.

"There must be an easier way," thought Coyote. Then it came to him. He was Coyote, after all, and he had many special powers given to him by the Great Spirit. So Coyote began to slowly take himself apart. He disconnected his ears, removed his nose and yanked off his feet, passing each piece through the small hole that Woodpecker had created. Coyote passed parts of his body through in this manner until every part of him was on the other side of the tree. Then he began to slowly reconstruct his body. He was almost done when he realized that he did not have his eyes. That pesky Raven had flown off with them, leaving Coyote blind and helpless.

Coyote searched about the forest floor for his eyes while all the animals laughed at his misfortune. It was then that Coyote came upon two pine cones. He picked them up and put them on in place of his eyes. He could not see anything with the pine cones, but Coyote was not worried about that. He pushed on through the forest, feeling his way, hoping to come into contact with someone, when he heard a laugh coming from one of the trees. It was the laughter of Raven's cousin, Blackbird.

"You foolish, Coyote. Have you not learned to stay away from my cousin Raven?" said Blackbird. "He is a crafty and tricky character and will take anything from you if he can. You are now blind through your own arrogance."

"Blind!" scoffed Coyote. "I am not blind. I can see with even greater clarity than you, Blackbird. My new eyes can see everything you see as well as the world of the spirits. It truly is the most amazing thing I have ever witnessed. Too bad you are stuck with those beady little eyes because you will never see anything like this."

Naturally, Blackbird was curious and begged Coyote to lend him his eyes so that he could see the spirit world. Blackbird then took out his eyes and gave them to Coyote, who then replaced the pine cones with Blackbird's eyes. Coyote could now see just as well as he had before, and, of course, Blackbird could see nothing because the pine cones were useless.

"Foolish, Blackbird," said Coyote. "For your laughter when I was blind, it will be you who are condemned. I will turn you into a snail, so that it will be you who will crawl around on your belly, feeling your way along."

# The Evil Two-faced Spirit

ONCE THERE WAS A TIME when Coyote had one daughter and 10 sons. Coyote's daughter, whom he had named Snow Flower, was the most beautiful woman in all the lands. One day, she walked to the river to take a bath in a private area. After taking off her clothes, she walked into the water and began to wash. It was then that she noticed a strange-looking man watching her from the edge of the forest. She put her clothes back on and tried to escape, but the man was already upon her and carried her away through the woods with great speed.

The evil double-faced spirit, Ko'Koa, had abducted her. Snow Flower tried calling out to her brothers for help, but she was too far from their village. "I will break up my beaded necklace and drop the pieces so that my family will know where to find me," she thought. So as the evil spirit carried her away through the forest, every 10 paces she would drop a piece of her necklace. By the time she had run out of beads, they had arrived at the home of Ko'Koa, where he kept her captive.

Over the next few days, she tried to escape many times but could not because the evil spirit had one face in front and one in back, and both faces watched her at all times. The face in the front was that of a handsome man and had a genuine look of kindness and sympathy in his eyes. The other face was not so easy to look at. The teeth on this face were gnarled and sharp, the lips were thin and curled, the skin was white as snow and two eyes bulged out of the head. Each face had a different personality, with two distinct voices controlling the one body. The young woman decided to appeal to the front face of Ko'Koa in the hope of touching his heart with her words.

"Please let me go," said Snow Flower, gently touching his cheek. "My family will be worried. My father is a great and powerful man, and he would surely give you a great reward if you were to return me unharmed."

"You truly are the most beautiful woman," said the front face. "I would like to you to stay, but if you feel..."

THE EVIL TWO-FACED SPIRIT

"You are not going anywhere," barked the second face suddenly, turning his body around to look her in the eyes. "You are our prisoner. We will have our way with you, and if you fight, you will be torn to pieces. You will look upon my face as I make you mine. You will give birth to my child."

There was no escape from Snow Flower's captor, and in a few months, she gave birth to Ko'Koa's child. Ko'Koa left the house every day to hunt and locked Snow Flower inside. Her only joy came in taking care of her new child and in the occasional kindness shown to her by the face in the front. Her only hope was that her brothers would come to take her back.

Meanwhile, after waiting for his daughter to return, Coyote decided to send his eldest son out to search for her two days after her disappearance. For weeks, the eldest son searched the forest until he finally found the first piece of her necklace. He walked farther along the path hoping to see another piece, but it was days before he found the next bead. The evil spirit had been traveling so fast that he could cover great distances in only a moment. Coyote's son had continued in this manner for several months, when he finally came upon the evil spirit's home. There he found his sister and her child home alone.

"Dearest Brother, you must leave immediately! Ko'Koa is out hunting and could return any moment. If he were to find you here, he would surely tear you to pieces," she said, pleading for him to leave.

Her brother did as she requested, but it was too late. When Ko'Koa returned home, he sensed that someone had been there.

"I can smell human," said the evil face on the back of the head, the saliva from its mouth dripping to the ground. "Your family has arrived. We just might have another for dinner tonight."

She tried to convince the front face of Ko'Koa that no one had visited, but the evil spirit did not believe her. Ko'Koa ran from the house at top speed, following the scent of her brother. In a flash, he caught up with the eldest brother, tore his limbs from his body, pulled his head off his neck and placed the body parts outside his home.

After sometime, two other brothers were sent to look for their missing family members, but this time Coyote had given his sons two bows and a supply of arrows. After walking in the same direction their eldest brother had taken, they came upon the house of Ko'Koa.

The brothers found their sister outside the home. She had a rope tied around her leg that was tied to a tree with magic. There was no way for her to escape.

"Please, Brothers, leave here now while Ko'Koa is still out hunting. You are in danger every second you remain," said Snow Flower, pointing to the dried-up corpse of the eldest brother on display. "I cannot bear to lose my other brothers. Run!"

The brothers obeyed, but it was too late. When Ko'Koa returned, he knew someone had been in his home. "I smell humans again. Your relatives are going to make lovely decorations," laughed the evil face of Ko'Koa. Snow Flower tried to lie to Ko'Koa again, but he was a powerful spirit and could see through her deception. He sprinted through the forest with such speed that he set upon the brothers before they even saw him coming. They, too, were torn to pieces and placed beside their eldest brother to bake in the sun. The same thing happened to the remainder of her brothers. Not one of Coyote's sons was left alive.

For months, Coyote waited for the return of his children, but no news arrived. He soon began to fear the worst. He mourned the loss of his children and began to weep. For days, tears flowed from his eyes and pooled on the ground. When he looked down one day, he saw that his tears had mixed with the mud and had taken the shape of a baby boy. Coyote wrapped the shape in cedar bark, and in seven days, it transformed into a real child. He called the child Anthtine, which meant "one made from tears." As the boy grew older and noticed his father crying, he asked, "Why do you always cry? What has made you so sad?"

Coyote replied, "I have been shedding tears for my lost daughter and 10 missing sons. I do not know what has become of them, but I fear the worst. Long ago, your sister left to bathe in the river and never returned. I sent out your brothers to find her, but they did not return, either. You are all that remains for me in this world."

"Father, you must let me search for them and find out what has become of them. I have grown big and strong. I am made of you, Father, from your tears and the solid earth, so do not fear for my life," said Anthtine.

Coyote begged his son to remain, but Anthtine could not be dissuaded, and he left in search of his sister and brothers. For weeks, he scoured the surrounding lands until he finally came upon the house of the evil spirit Ko'Koa.

Remaining in the cover of the woods, Anthtine scanned the clearing for any signs of danger. Off in the distance, he could see his sister tending to her chores, and though they seemed to be covered in shadows, Anthtine saw the outlines of all his brothers. A great feeling of joy swept through him. He ran out of the woods and approached his sister.

"Brothers and Sister, I have come to…" began Anthtine, but his words were cut short when the shadows lifted and he saw the dried corpses of his brothers. "What horror is this?!" he cried.

Startled by the appearance of this stranger, Snow Flower asked, "Who are you? What do you want?"

"I am the son of your father. I have come to rescue you and kill whatever has done this to my brothers!" cried out Anthtine. "Please tell me how I can kill him."

She replied in a whisper, "You must wait until Ko'Koa is asleep. That is when his heart comes out of his chest. If you stab at him then, he will certainly die. Come back tonight, and I will leave the door open so that you can sneak in unnoticed. But please run at top speed far away from here because Ko'Koa will soon be home, and if he finds you, you will most certainly end up with your brothers."

That evening when Ko'Koa returned from the hunt, his child called out, "Mother had a visitor." When Ko'Koa heard this, he immediately sped out along the path and caught up to Anthtine. Ko'Koa grabbed him by the throat and was about to rip off his head when, suddenly, Anthtine simply disappeared. Ko'Koa frantically searched for him with all four eyes but still could not find him. But suddenly Anthtine reappeared. Ko'Koa pursued Anthtine again, but every time Ko'Koa came close, Anthtine disappeared. Frustrated, Ko'Koa gave up. "This one has been given powers by a very magical spirit. I must get my rest before I can taste his flesh," said the evil face to himself. He then returned to his home to rest.

Anthtine remained hidden in the forest until nightfall. He then crept quietly up to the house and peered through a knothole in one of the walls. He could see that Ko'Koa's heart was on the evil spirit's chest. Snow Flower lay next to Ko'Koa with their child in her arms. Anthtine quietly crept through the unlocked door and stabbed Ko'Koa's heart, killing him instantly.

The child of Ko'Koa began to scream and suddenly grew an evil face on the back of his head, just like his father. "Kill my child quickly before he becomes like his father," Snow Flower said to Anthtine, and Anthtine killed the child as well. Anthtine and his sister then returned home to their father Coyote, and many days of celebration followed.

# Coyote Meets Raven and Lynx

ONE DAY, RAVEN STOLE a piece of meat and settled down on a branch of a tree to eat his prize. Passing by, Coyote caught sight of him and made up his mind to take the meat from Raven.

Looking up into the branches, Coyote said as loudly as he could, "What a fine and elegant creature! Surely, Raven, you deserve to be the king of all birds. I bet you would be the king if only you could sing."

Raven, never one to let a challenge go unfulfilled, was overly anxious to show Coyote that he did indeed possess a voice that could crown him king of all birds. He let out a loud "Caw!"—and the meat dropped to the ground.

"Ah, Raven," said Coyote as he rushed over to pick up his prize, "I see now that you were not lacking in a beautiful voice but only common sense," and he simply walked away.

After eating his meal, Coyote then happened upon the boastful Lynx. Lynx would always say that he was the most beautiful animal in the forest. Coyote knew with certainty that he was the best-looking creature and could not allow the Lynx to continue with the lies. Yet, no matter how many times Coyote claimed he was more beautiful, Lynx came back saying, "I am surely more beautiful than you, Coyote. Just look at the intricate design of my coat."

Tired of Lynx's incessant bragging, Coyote finally said, "But I am surely more beautiful than you—for it is my mind that is intricate, not merely my coat."

# Coyote Moves the Heavens

IN A TIME LONG BEFORE the memory of our people, there lived a young Coyote. He lived in a beautiful valley near a swift-running river filled with tasty salmon for him to eat. Coyote spent his days eating his fill and laying in the sunshine. He was the master of his world and seemed content with his place in it, never once questioning how things came to be or if there were other beings in the world. Coyote was happy in his universe and never felt the need to share. Sharing was not natural for him. But in time, Coyote became more curious about the world beyond his valley meadow and the many fun things he might do beyond the world around him.

"What if there were other animals? What if I had someone to play with, or someone to do work for me, hmm?" thought Coyote devilishly.

Coyote quickly put those thoughts to the side once his stomach loudly echoed its displeasure at being empty. He lazily lifted himself off his patch of grass under the sun, stretched out his long, skinny legs and let out a monstrous yawn. Wandering down to the edge of the river, Coyote looked into the water and saw that the salmon occupied almost every space. This was the normal way of things at the time. The salmon were so plentiful that he simply had to put his mouth under the water, and he would come up with a catch. But, for the first time, Coyote wondered, "What else is there to eat in this world? Surely there are things other than simple salmon that can satisfy my hunger."

Coyote had never followed the course of the river nor ever wondered where it flowed, but first, he had to satisfy his appetite. He had his fill of salmon and, after a long nap, he followed the waters toward the western edge of the valley. When he first began his journey along the river, the blue waters remained calm, but as he got closer and closer to the valley's edge, the waters began to churn and crash with such violence that the air filled with mist. He also noticed a figure moving in the haze of the raging waters along the other side of the river. Its shape resembled that of Coyote himself but was much smaller and moved a lot faster.

"I'm late, I'm late," called the voice. "I'm late. Now I must go. No time...No time."

Coyote strained his keen eyes to see through the mist and was just able to catch a glimpse of a red tail with a black tip. Coyote instantly became excited. "Who was this red stranger and from where could he have come?" wondered Coyote. Since time began, Coyote had explored every part of the valley but had never encountered another soul.

"Wait, stranger!" Coyote yelled over the thunder of the river. "I would like to meet you...Wait!"

"You must then cross the river if you want to travel with me, but do hurry for we are all terribly late," replied the stranger.

Coyote looked but did not see any possible way of getting across the river without being pulled down into the rushing waters where he would surely drown. Looking around frantically for something to help him cross the river, his eyes came to rest on a tree that had been hollowed out by time. "This will be safe for me to cross the river in," said Coyote out loud to himself in an attempt to muster the courage to face the torrent.

"I'm late!" yelled the voice with the red tail.

Coyote leapt into the hollowed-out tree and pushed off from the banks of the river. Although the tree managed to stay afloat, it got caught in a swift current and put Coyote on a direct path with a large, swirling void where the waters simply disappeared. Despite the thrashing of his make-shift boat, with the water crashing down upon him, Coyote caught a glimpse of the stranger with the red tail disappearing into the mists. Before Coyote even had time to take another breath, the boat crashed into a large rapid, and he was thrown into the raging torrent.

Instead of feeling the overwhelming sensation of drowning, Coyote felt almost as if he was falling through a liquid sky. Yet he felt no sense of danger, no sense of suffocating. In this tumbling, swirling universe, he fell into a serene peace before his journey came to an abrupt halt. When he opened his eyes, he found himself in the strangest of landscapes.

The first thing Coyote noticed was what he was standing on—it was not upon dirt or rock that his feet rested but on rolling white clouds that looked just like the clouds in the sky. Coyote got to his feet unsteadily and surveyed the new world he had entered. Looking up, he saw that he was in the center of some sort of cloud forest. He could see the shapes of trees, bushes and rocks, but they were all wrapped in layers of swirling clouds. Then something else caught his eye. Behind a tree, he saw the red tail of the animal that had led him to this place. Coyote made his way to the tree and jumped on the red-tailed stranger. Once the animal was firmly in his grasp, Coyote looked through the clouds and saw that he had caught an animal not unlike himself.

"Who are you, stranger?" Coyote demanded.

"Why, I am Fox, of course," screeched the stranger. "But I am late. You don't understand—if I'm late, I will lose my head."

Fox looked very similar to Coyote, except that he was much smaller and his fur was a different color. "Why, in the name of the Great Spirit, would you lose your head?" asked Coyote. "You look very much like me—we must be related. If you are in need, Brother, I will surely come to your aid. Tell me your story."

Fox sat down, and Coyote listened as he recounted his story.

"For as long as there has been a universe, we have been held captive here by an evil, old witch. She allows me to go free to run her errands sometimes because I am small and fast, but I and all the other animals of the Great Spirit's creation have been trapped under the tyranny of this most vile hag since the beginning of time," said Fox. "She is the most hideous of creatures and holds us prisoner because she does not want anyone to compare our beauty with her ugliness. Every night, the witch wails into the black night, cursing her misfortune and raging at the Great Spirit for making everyone beautiful except her. We suffer a great deal under her guard and are tortured nearly every night. We thought we were the only beings in this whole place, but when I stumbled upon you in the valley, I knew you were here to help us. You don't remember, do you?"

"Remember what?" asked Coyote.

"You once were a prisoner of the old witch, but you escaped using your gift of cunning. This was so long ago that you must have forgotten. All those comfortable days in the valley getting fat on salmon and lying out in the sun have clouded your mind. I have been looking for you for so long while out on my errands. Now you can show us how you escaped and help the others."

"I do not remember ever escaping, but if I did it once, then I can surely do it again. But, dear Fox, you are free now, so why do you not simply run away?" asked Coyote.

"I only wish it were true. Although I walk free, I am bound to return because of an evil magic spell," said Fox. "I must go now, but you will help us escape, Brother. Follow me through the cloud forest to the land of shadows in which she dwells and see the horrors her evil has wrought, then you will truly understand, for sometimes in seeing only then do we hear the truth."

Fox grabbed hold of Coyote, threw him on his back and sped through the forest at lightning speed. Fox's feet barely touched the ground, but he moved faster than Coyote could ever run. Fox darted through the cloud forest with skillful grace and only slowed down once they came to a clearing. Along the horizon, Coyote could see that the bright clouds gradually disappeared, as if slowly being swallowed by the land of shadows.

"You must travel this last road on your own. I must return. If I don't, she will send some evil magic after me," said Fox. "You must do what you can to help us." With those last words, Fox disappeared in a blur, and all Coyote could see was a red streak headed directly into darkness.

Coyote sat and stared into the dark lands before him and tried to remember the days when he was trapped in this place. But his memories had faded with time. The past didn't matter to Coyote for he was the most cunning creature and would have no problem fooling the witch one more time, even if he didn't remember anything. He decided to disguise himself in human form as a traveler, with a bag over his shoulder and a large cloak with a hood that hid his face—that way he might be able to gain access to the evil hag's lodge and free the prisoners. Transforming into the traveler, Coyote set out along the path toward the land of shadows.

As he entered into the land of shadows, all light suddenly disappeared. Even the bright light of the cloud forest was swallowed by the darkness. The only source of illumination came from a large fire off in the distance that cast faint shadows across the landscape, revealing a world devoid of life and beauty.

Coyote made his way through the barren terrain with only the dim light from the fire as his guide. In time, he finally arrived at the camp of the old witch. Taking a deep breath, Coyote knocked on the door.

"Bah, who dares come to my door," growled the voice from inside. "Arrr, I'm busy. Go away!"

"Please open the door," said Coyote. "I'm just a tired traveler. I have been without sleep for days on end, and I would like nothing more than a place to rest my head."

"Go away!" repeated the voice.

"Please, my lady. I'm weary with travel, and I have a great many stories to tell you," said Coyote. "I just came from a wonderful valley that was bathed in sunshine. It had a river full of salmon and was home to a curious creature named Coyote."

With those final words, the lodge fell silent. After a minute, the door slowly creaked open, revealing the inside of the evil witch's lair. "Enter, traveler!" she bellowed. "And close the door behind you."

Swallowing his fear, Coyote, still disguised as the traveler, walked through the doorway. The only source of light in the room was a small fire used for cooking, and there was just enough light falling across the room that Coyote could make out the old hag's features.

Although he tried not to look upon her in shock, his muscles betrayed his emotions and he could not help from frowning at the sight of her face. Her skin was green, stained with brown and had the texture of a dirt path. Her giant nose hooked out from her face, and from its very tip protruded a large wart, which, when Coyote stared at it, seemed to pulsate. Her teeth were nearly black with filth, and her hot breath filled the room with the most acrid smell. Her hands were the size of Coyote's head, and her fingernails looked like jagged daggers.

"Tell me of this Coyote," the witch said with a growl.

"I met this most distinguished of animals when I was traveling through a lovely valley. He was lying out in the sun after having eaten his fill of salmon, and he invited me to talk with him. He then told me how he had escaped from the most revolting hag he had ever seen," said Coyote, watching the witch's face turn red with anger.

"That insolent dog! He is my trophy! He belongs to me and has no business out in the world. Fox, come here!" she shouted.

Fox came scurrying into the room but was hampered by a large chain secured tightly around his neck. He kept his head bowed toward the floor but lifted his sad eyes to meet those of the stranger.

"I send you out on these errands, and you fail to bring me news of Coyote. You stupid little runt!" screamed the hag, yanking on the chain and forcing Fox to his knees. "You were just in the same valley as this stranger, and you did not report to me that you saw Coyote. I have been looking for that beast ever since he escaped from me. You useless Fox! Now get back in your cage."

Fox slowly walked out of the room, but before disappearing, he took one look back at Coyote and gave him a wink.

"I can tell you how to get to Coyote, but the journey is long. I can stay here and watch over your lodge for you. But be warned that Coyote is a cunning character and will certainly do what he can to hold on to his freedom," explained the traveler.

Although the hag did not trust the traveler, the lure of getting back her most prized captive was too difficult to resist. Coyote's plan was working. "Do not worry, gracious hostess. I will simply lay down here and rest my weary legs," said Coyote. Then, adding to his deception, he gave the hag the wrong directions for how to reach the valley. Coyote knew it would not be long before she realized that she had been fooled, but he only needed a short time to free the others.

The old hag quickly gathered some supplies and darted out the door into the darkness. The earth shook beneath the hag's feet as she plodded away from the lodge. When her footsteps could no longer be heard, Coyote transformed into his original form and opened the door from which Fox had earlier emerged.

Inside, Coyote found a most horrible sight. Entering a large, cave-like room, Coyote could just see by the light of the torch the faint shadows of all the animals the Great Spirit had ever created. They lay on the floor joined together by a single large, heavy chain. Each animal was attached to the chain by a golden lock that was held in place by powerful magic. Unable to move, and clearly weak from mistreatment, the animals' faces lit up at seeing Coyote.

"You have returned!" exclaimed Bear.

"Coyote, we have missed you," said Eagle.

"Thank the Great Spirit," professed Deer.

Coyote looked deeper into the room and saw all the animals of the world shackled together in a similar manner. There was Beaver, Otter, Blue Jay, Mink, Fox, Moose, Mountain Lion, Wolf, Rabbit and many more. Coyote had to rub his eyes to make sure he was not seeing an illusion.

"Do you remember me?" asked Coyote.

"We sure do," replied Rabbit. "We have been looking for you ever since you left us so long ago. Why did you forget us?"

"I can't remember those days spent here. It must have been put out of my mind once I arrived in the valley and became lost in the beauty and ease of my surroundings," said Coyote.

At hearing this, Bear stood on his hind legs and shouted, "You left us here to rot, only to gorge yourself on salmon and sleep away the day under the sun! I should tear your head off and give it as a trophy to the old hag—maybe then she would let us go."

Coyote was not surprised that he had abandoned the other animals for the peace and plenty of the valley, but he knew of a way to make up for his actions.

"I am very sorry, my dear friends," pleaded Coyote. "I should never have left you here. My memory had truly faded. But that is the past. I shall make it up to you now by releasing you from these golden shackles before the evil hag returns—and don't worry, she will forever remember this day."

With those words, all the animals let forth a loud cheer. Coyote at once used his magic to break the golden bonds, and all the animals poured out into the land of shadows. Coyote was busy gathering up all the golden locks that had held the animals when he heard a cry from outside.

"The hag!" cried Eagle. "I can see her off in the distance, and she doesn't look happy. We need to hurry."

But Coyote continued to gather the golden locks.

"Coyote, hurry!" said Fox. "We need to run for she will surely be back any minute. I know of the place where we can escape this world and return to earth, but you must hurry."

But Coyote was still preoccupied with the golden chains. "Don't worry, Fox. I have a little gift for the old witch to remember us by."

It was then that Coyote took the golden locks and threw them up into the pitch-black sky. Far into the dark sky the shining pieces of metal went before finally coming to rest. But Coyote's aim was not random, for he had left a gift for the old hag. All the stars in the sky were placed with purpose and reason—each individual star connected to other stars to form the shape of every single animal she had captured. If you trace a line between each star, you will clearly see the outlines of animals such as Buffalo and Fox, and, of course, the biggest and brightest of all, Coyote.

Coyote had just finished placing the stars when the old hag descended upon the lodge.

Quickly surveying the area, her blood-shot eyes caught sight of the animals' chains strewn across her yard, and she knew at once what had happened. "I have been taken for a fool!" she cried. Looking around her for the culprit, she spotted Coyote and Fox sprinting toward the cloud forest.

It was then that her horrid face stared directly into the sky and saw what had become of her golden locks. Her anguished wailing chilled the animals to the bone, but Coyote simply smiled. Stopping to admire his handiwork, Coyote called back at the old witch, "I have made this beautiful sky to remind you, old hag, of the evil you wrought upon the innocent creatures of the Great Spirit.

Each day when you look up, you will remember that there is beauty in this world and that your ugliness is the result of the evil within you. Remember this day, witch, and that it was Coyote who fooled you. It shall be this way for all eternity."

With those final words, Coyote disappeared into the mists of the cloud forest and joined the other animals all gathered around a black hole in the ground. Although out of danger, they could still hear the tortured moans of the hag as she looked up at the new stars in the sky.

"All right," said Fox, "everyone into the hole. Quickly now, before the hag closes the door with her magic."

Coyote was the first to jump in, followed by Buffalo, Fox and Deer. The last animal to go was Beaver. Never one to move too fast on land, Beaver slowly walked up to the hole but, just as he was about to jump in, the old hag suddenly came running up and threw a magic herb over the opening. Beaver saw that the hole was beginning to close up, and though he escaped, his round, fat tail got flattened on its way through the hole.

Down the hole the animals went, tumbling through the air. But, as when Coyote had fallen in the first time, there was no fear, no sense of falling toward solid ground—there was only the rush of air over their faces and the knowledge that they were now free.

One by one the animals appeared from the sky and landed safely on earth. Buffalo ran off to the open plains to feed on the lush grasses. Bear ran to the river to feed on salmon. Eagle took to the sky and settled on his mountain perch, and Rabbit scurried down into his burrow to escape the sun.

Coyote was content knowing that he had outsmarted the old witch and freed the animals. As the sun began to descend behind the mountains, Coyote howled toward the sky and watched as the thousands of stars he had thrown into the heavens suddenly came to life. After such an exhausting day, Coyote had his fill of salmon, lay his head down in the lush grass and fell asleep once more.

# Coyote and the Frog Women

COYOTE WAS VERY LONELY. He had no wife and no friends. So one day he decided he would follow the river to the coast to fetch some salmon. Coyote packed a few supplies and began the long journey to the coast. After two days of walking through pouring rain and whipping winds, he was feeling very tired and stopped to take a rest. It was then that he came upon two Frog women digging into the ground looking for roots to eat.

"Hello, Coyote," they said in unison. "Where are you going?"

Coyote did not answer because he was too tired and wanted nothing to do with the Frog women, but the pests insisted on bothering him.

"Come on, Coyote, tell us where you're going. We want to know," they said again.

Coyote pretended that he did not hear them, but the two women would not give up, and they repeated their question.

"Fine! What do you Frogs want?!" screamed Coyote.

"We want nothing in particular. Where are you headed?" they asked again.

"I'm going to the coast to find salmon to eat, if you must know," said Coyote.

"Oh, salmon! We would love us some salmon. Can you bring us back some when you pass through here next time?" the Frog women begged. "We are tired of digging for dry, bitter roots. We have not tasted flesh in weeks," said one of the Frog women, her lips dripping with saliva.

Coyote knew that the women would never leave him alone if he did not agree. "I will gladly drop off some salmon on my way back through here," he said, walking off again along the river.

As Coyote continued his journey, he thought of ways he could play some sort of trick on the annoying Frogs. He wanted to devise a trick the like of which had never been done before, but nothing special came to mind, for he knew the Frog women were very clever and could not be easily fooled.

It was at this time that Coyote came upon a nest of bees. He whispered to the bees that the Frog women had said bad things about their queen, and the two women would kill her if they had the chance. The bees vowed they would use their stingers to punish the women for saying such things. Coyote told the bees to hide in his pack, and when he gave them the signal, they were to jump out and sting the Frog women. The bees flew into Coyote's sack, and he then slung the pack over his shoulder and returned to where he had last seen the Frog women.

The women were in the same place, digging at the same hole, when they spotted Coyote coming from a distance. "Here comes our friend, Sister. Look over there," said one.

"He better have brought us some salmon," said the other.

"Hey, Coyote! Over here! Do you know us?" they called out.

Coyote had seen them, but he purposely continued to walk and did not acknowledge their existence. The women hopped over to Coyote and pulled at his coat. "Coyote. It is us—the Frog women. Did you bring us some tasty treats? Are they in your pack?

Can we have some?" they both said, grabbing at the pack slung over his shoulder.

Coyote gently took the pack off his back and placed it on the ground before him. "Now, ladies, you can both stick your heads into the pack, and you will find the most delectable salmon you have ever tasted. I caught you several salmon each," said Coyote.

The Frog women slipped their heads inside the pack, and Coyote gave it a swift kick to anger the bees even more. He then sealed the sack over their heads, and the bees killed the two women with 1000 poisonous stings. After the women died, Coyote removed their private parts and took them with him. Whenever he wanted, he could take their privates and use them as he pleased. That is why Coyote sometimes howls at night.

The two Frog women eventually came back to life and found out that Coyote had stolen their private parts. This is why it is said among the people that the reason female frogs do not have private parts is because Coyote has still not given them back.

# Into the Well

ONE BLISTERING HOT DAY, Coyote came upon a natural well filled with cool water. Extremely thirsty, he did not pay attention to the ever-present danger of falling into the well as he approached it for a drink. Not watching his footing, Coyote fell into the well and could not get out.

It was some time before a thirsty Sheep peered over the edge and, on seeing Coyote, asked whether the water was good to drink. Ever cunning, Coyote hid his distress and eloquently celebrated the quality of the water and invited Sheep to join him for a refreshing drink. Sheep, at great risk to himself, managed to clamber down into the well, and after drinking his fill, consulted with Coyote as to the best way of getting out of their predicament.

"It will be easy if we just help each other," said Coyote. "Just brace your powerful legs against the side and raise your head up as high as you can. I will then climb over you, and when I have freed myself, I will pull you out."

Seeing the obvious logic in Coyote's plan, Sheep agreed. Coyote scrambled up Sheep's back and head and used his horns as a ladder to climb up over the edge of the well. Coyote then disappeared from sight.

Sheep was furious over the sudden turn of events and loudly berated Coyote for not keeping his end of the bargain. Coyote turned back, leaned over the edge of the well and said, "Look, friend, if your head was good for anything besides sprouting those horns, you would have known better than to get into a well without having a way to get yourself out." And with that, Coyote walked away, leaving Sheep to his fate.

# To the Moon

AT ONE TIME, COYOTE lived along the Columbia River with his wife and two children. It was a wonderful place to live, and his family had plenty of food to eat. There were mountain sheep for him to hunt and salmon in the river to catch.

Early one morning, Coyote gathered up his hunting gear, said goodbye to his family and traveled into the mountains in search of his next meal. After traveling for nearly a full day to the hunting grounds, he built a camp and went to sleep for the night.

The next day, Coyote was woken by the mocking sounds of laughter. Jumping to his feet, he looked around for the source of the disturbance and found Raven perched high up in a tree cackling out his song.

"What is the meaning of this?!" cried out Coyote. "Why are you disturbing me when I'm on the hunt?"

"Caw! Caw!" laughed Raven. "Foolish Coyote, if you had glorious wings like mine, you could fly into the air and see your prey from above. But you remain bound to the earth like a little worm."

"Be gone, little pest. I have no time for your games," replied Coyote.

"If you had wings, you would have all the time in the world. Caw! Caw! Caw!" taunted Raven. "You're not a very powerful spirit if you cannot fly. The Great Spirit surely did not favor your kind."

Coyote tried to ignore the taunts of Raven, but he could not help being jealous of the black bird and his ability to fly. Coyote packed up his camp and continued on his way to the mountain, hoping to forget the Raven, but the annoying black bird's laughter could be heard throughout the region.

"If there was some way for me to fly, I would surely show that bird who the champion of the sky is," thought Coyote.

He tried to put that morning's annoyance out of his mind, but as he neared the hunting grounds, he still couldn't stop thinking of what he could accomplish if he could soar through the air. How high could he fly? How far could he go?

Although distracted, he still managed to sneak up on a large sheep and kill it with one shot from his bow. After skinning the animal, Coyote laid the skin out on a large rock to dry in the hot sun. Looking at the sheep's hide, he suddenly had an idea. "What if I were to blow into the sheep's skin and capture the air inside? Maybe I could fly!"

Once the sheep's skin was dry enough, Coyote sewed the edges together, leaving only a small opening. Taking a deep breath, he blew and blew inside the sheep's skin until it was twice the size of its original form. Taking one last breath, Coyote blew as hard as he could. But he blew a little too hard, because the skin suddenly exploded, knocking Coyote off his feet. Of course, Raven was nearby to witness the explosion and started to laugh at Coyote's misfortune.

"Silly dog. Only we birds have been blessed with flight. Stop your insane attempts, Coyote. You'll never be able to soar in the sky with us," said Raven, who took off into the air and continued his mocking laughter until he disappeared from sight.

Raven's laughter served only to double Coyote's resolve, and after killing another sheep, he set about the same experiment yet again. This time, he was a little more careful. Coyote took a special magic powder and dusted it over the skin before blowing it up. With each breath he exhaled into the skin, it began to lift off the ground. With a few more puffs, it was fully inflated. Now that the skin was lighter, Coyote had to tie it down to a boulder so it would not float away. It was when he was looking up at the sky that he saw the moon and wondered what it would be like to visit the people that lived there.

"Surely Raven has never flown that high," Coyote thought. "If I were able to bring something back from the people that lived there, then everyone would praise me for my bravery and cunning."

Coyote then fashioned a basket out of reeds and attached it to the floating sheepskin. Climbing into the basket, Coyote cut the basket loose from the boulder and soared high into the sky. He closed his eyes at first, but he was quickly overcome with the excitement of flying in the air. He flew up above the forests, soaring over the mountain peaks before bursting through the clouds. Up he rose, getting farther and farther away from his homeland. Coyote now was so high that he could see straight to the coast to the vast expanse of water that stretched until it fell on the other side of the earth. When he looked up, he could no longer see the blue sky, only a vast darkness and an ivory moon floating before his eyes.

Closer and closer he got to the moon, and just as he had watched the earth shrink into the distance, the moon began to envelope the horizon as he came in to land. Landing in a rough, dusty clearing, Coyote could see a series of houses off in the distance with smoke billowing from their chimneys. He walked into one of the houses and saw walls covered in the most intricate and beautiful baskets. From behind one wall came the faintest of lights, piercing through the cracks between the baskets, and Coyote could hear the whispers of a group of women. As Coyote reached out to remove one of the baskets, a voice called out from the darkness.

"Do not touch what is not yours," warned the voice. "If you steal anything, you will never be able to leave this place."

The warning sent a chill through Coyote. He dropped the basket and walked straight out of the house. It was strange, thought Coyote, that he could hear activity inside the houses, but not a single person could be seen outside. A light wind swept through the tiny village, blowing open the door to a house across from the one he had just left. Coyote walked into the home and once again could not find a single soul but could only hear the voices of women quietly whispering. The walls of this house were covered with ornate and colorful mats of all sizes. Coyote wondered where the people of this strange land that seemed devoid of colors had learned to create things of such beauty. He could not help picking one of the mats off the wall, but again, the moment he touched the mat, a voice sounded from the darkness, "Do not touch what is not yours, or else you shall never return to your family."

"Never, never steal," called out another voice.

"Okay, I will not take what is not mine," replied Coyote.

Almost running out the door, Coyote traveled to the house farthest from the others and peered in through the door, afraid of what might await him inside. Instead of finding an evil monster, Coyote came across an elderly couple huddled around a fire.

"Come in, young man," said the old man. "You must be a traveler because I have never laid my eyes upon someone like yourself. You must be weary. Please sit with us."

Relieved at finally finding a welcoming home, Coyote sat next to the fire and warmed his aching bones.

"Ever since I can remember, I have always wanted to come to this land. When I look up in the sky from my world, your home fully shines down upon ours every 29 days," said Coyote.

"This is indeed a large land, stranger, but we have certain rules in this place that must be followed by all visitors," replied the old woman. "Follow them, or pay the consequences. Now please eat with us, as there is nothing left for you to do since you cannot go home."

"Why can I not return home? My craft still functions, and I obeyed the rules of this place," said Coyote.

"You did indeed, but this is a magical place, and we are bound by its rules. No one may travel while your home cannot be seen in the sky," said the old man. "But be warned, time passes slowly in this world, and when you do return home, things might be different."

"For now you will stay far away from the other houses here. The ones that live inside them cannot be seen and are angered quickly if disturbed," warned the old woman.

"If it must be, then I will stay," said Coyote.

Coyote was unsure of just how long he had spent with his guests, but he passed his days helping the elderly couple with their daily chores. As time

COYOTE TALES OF THE NORTHWEST

passes more slowly on the moon than on earth, Coyote had only been with the strangers for 28 days, but it actually felt like he had been away for two years. Every day, he gladly helped the elderly couple, but in the still of the evening, his thoughts turned to his family and his homeland.

One night, the old woman approached Coyote. "You are very lonely here," she said. "You miss your family, don't you?"

"I miss the warmth of my wife and the love of my children," replied Coyote.

"Weep not, for you will be leaving us tomorrow. We will suffer in your absence, but we will always remember your kindness," sobbed the old woman. "You have learned much while you have been here, so in return for your help, I present you with these gifts."

The old woman handed him some berries and meat for the journey home. She gave Coyote instructions on how to make the baskets and mats that the people of the moon were so expert in creating. She also imparted to him the wisdom of how to make arrowheads, how to dry salmon and how to cook meat using fire.

"We want you to take these things and pass on our knowledge to the people of your world," said the old woman.

Coyote agreed and retired to his bed early, eager to leave in the morning.

When he woke, he found that the elderly couple had already prepared his sheepskin balloon and air basket. Once Coyote was inside the basket, the elderly woman explained how he was to guide his craft safely home. "You must continually tap the bottom of your basket with your foot and command the craft in a soft whisper to go lower, lower, lower," she said. "Now take all that we have taught you and pass it on to others. You will be missed, noble Coyote."

Just as the basket lifted off the ground, a tear rolled down the old woman's cheek and fell into the basket.

Lifting off the surface of the moon, Coyote tapped his foot and softly commanded the basket, "Lower, lower, lower," and he started to make the journey back to earth. Coyote looked at the moon and waved to the elderly couple who had taken care of him. But the surface of the moon quickly began to fall away, and Coyote soon sailed into the blue skies of earth. He could make out the vast blue ocean along the coast and the mountain ranges he called home. "Lower, lower, lower...," Coyote called out while tapping his foot even faster in a rush to get home. As the basket coasted over the mountains and made its descent into the same valley from where he had departed, Coyote could see Raven watching from his perch in a tree.

"I have proven you a fool, Raven. I truly am the smartest and most cunning, for I have been to the land of the moon and have returned with great amounts of knowledge," said Coyote, holding his head high.

Raven could say nothing in return because Coyote had proven that he could soar higher than any creature had ever done; all he could do was watch as Coyote landed. After unloading all the gifts, Coyote looked up at the moon and felt a sudden sadness at having left the elderly couple. A tear rolled down his cheek and fell into the basket. The moment Coyote's tear hit the basket, the craft suddenly lifted into the air and flew back to the moon.

A voice then spoke to Coyote, "You have shed a tear for us as we did when you left us. From this moment forward, the clouds will cry, and you will call it 'rain.'"

Although Coyote had been gone for only a month, he had aged two years, and he thought no one in his village would recognize him, but as he climbed the path to his house, his children immediately recognized him. After Coyote greeted his children and his wife, a large meal was prepared, and everyone ate their fill. After the meal, Coyote told them about his adventures. He told them about Raven laughing at him, about the sheepskin craft, about leaving the earth and about landing on the moon.

"The people on the moon are not like we are here, but they are kind and have shown me many things that I will now share with you. First of all, they do not eat their food raw. They use fire to prepare their meals."

Coyote's family was astonished by this information and at first did not believe that people could control fire. But Coyote told his children to gather some dried birch bark and twigs and showed them how to create a spark by rubbing two sticks together. Coyote then took a rock and placed it in the fire. When the rock was hot, he removed it and dropped it into one of the baskets he had been given that was filled with water. Instantly, the water began to boil. He then dropped in the meat, and it was cooked in a few minutes. His wife immediately called together all the people of the village to learn the secrets of the people of the moon. Coyote taught them to weave baskets, to make mats and to cook with fire, thereby passing on the knowledge he had been given.

Many years later, Coyote looked up at the moon and wondered what had happened to the people, when he heard a voice call out to him.

"Coyote, there is no one living here any longer. Only shadows. One day, if someone was to return, they would find nothing but dust. Do not weep for us, for our people live on through the knowledge we have passed down to you."

# Coyote Rattles Some Bones

Long ago when the land was open and free, Coyote roamed through the valleys and over the mountains looking for something that could entertain him for the moment. Coyote was a curious character and always found something to do, but for weeks he had seen no one. There were no birds in the sky and no deer roaming the forests.

"What land have I entered?" he thought to himself. "There is no life in the air nor on the ground."

But as he was curious by nature, Coyote went farther into this desolate place that was only covered by tall, yellow grass. The grass towered over Coyote's head, obstructing the view, but he had been walking on very well-marked paths that radiated out from some central point. He followed one of the paths until it led him into a vast, flat plain. There was no grass, no trees, no rocks, just pile after pile of bones, thousands of them. Coyote then knew that he had wandered into a graveyard.

But by the time he entered a clearing, the sun had set and an evening mist rolled through the graveyard. Coyote walked among the bones to get a better look at them, but the darkness obscured his sight.

"Dead Brothers, hear my song. Come back to this world and tell me your story. I have not seen anyone in a long time, and I need to be entertained." Coyote continued to sing his tune into the night sky when suddenly, all the bones began to rattle. Then came a voice out of the darkness.

"Why do you disturb us, Coyote? What is so important that you have called the dead back to their bones?"

"I have not seen a person on this earth for many weeks, and I was beginning to wonder if everyone had left. So I found you and brought you back," said Coyote.

"What a foolish reason to disturb a dusty pile of bones! Coyote, we shall rise and kill you for disturbing our slumber," said the booming voice.

The bones rattled again and slowly come to life. Coyote watched as thousands of bones put themselves back together, piece by piece: first the feet, then the hips, then the spine and finally the head. Coyote had found the graveyard of the moose.

"You cannot kill me—you are just made of bones. I am the great Coyote. I am and have always been. Nothing can harm me. You can't even catch me," Coyote exclaimed with confidence.

Without another word, the moose bones shook once more, chased Coyote out of the graveyard and pursued him across the valley. Coyote was much faster than the moose, but the lumbering giants were persistent and did not need to rest. Coyote could run ahead, have time to eat a meal and take a nap before the moose could catch up. This race continued for days, then weeks until Coyote finally began to tire. The moose were still charging forward and showed no signs of stopping. Eventually, Coyote collapsed on the ground and gave in to the moose.

"Peace, Brothers, peace. Let us make some sort of deal that will see all of us happy. I will fix you and bring you back to life so that you might once again roam the forests and eat all the greens you want."

"If we agree, and you trick us, we will pursue you for all eternity," warned the moose.

So Coyote began the long process of bringing the moose back to life. He gave each one a thick coat of fur, a strong back and legs as tall as trees. He then lined their bodies with thick layers of muscle and fat.

"Now you are formidable opponents for any creature in the forest, but something is missing," said Coyote. "I know…weapons upon your heads."

Coyote searched through the forest for something to place upon the heads of the moose. He found some branches of a pine tree and put them on the head of one of the moose.

"Now I want you to run into that rock and test the strength of these branches," ordered Coyote.

The moose did as instructed, and the branches on his head were smashed into thousands of little pieces.

Coyote searched through the forest for something else that could withstand the power behind the moose and deliver devastating blows to their enemies. He found the branches of a fir tree, but the wood was still too soft.

"I have been looking in the wrong place," said Coyote. He then walked up to a mountain and carved a pair of branches out of stone, which he then placed on the head of one of the moose.

"This is what you need. You now have antlers," said Coyote. He carved thousands of antlers from the stone of the mountain and placed them on the heads of all the male moose. When Coyote was finished, he had carved so many antlers from the mountains that he created the Okanagan Valley.

The moose were so happy with the way they looked that the chief of the Moose tribe came forth and made an offer. "You have helped us greatly, Coyote, and for that we will repay you with kindness, too."

At that time, Coyote was said to look very different than he does now. His legs were short, his eyes were round and his nose was pushed in. So the moose chief grabbed Coyote and spun him around several times by his legs, and Coyote's legs stretched out and became long and skinny. The chief then pulled on Coyote's nose until it became long and his eyes stretched to become tiny slits. Then moose gave him a new coat of fur.

"You look much better, Coyote. To thank you for helping us and making us whole again, we will make you a member of the moose tribe," said the moose chief.

Coyote now was no longer lonely, for everywhere he went, the moose followed him, but Coyote decided he could not stay. The moose were always together, and Coyote could never find time to be alone. So one night, Coyote left the tribe, and since then has not joined any other tribe but his own.

# Ride the Shooting Star

LONG AGO, COYOTE HAD been doing many good deeds across the lands when he stopped to take stock of his accomplishments and brag about all that he had done.

"I am the great Coyote, the most powerful spirit of this world. I have defeated monsters and made fire for the people. I have moved mountains and traveled to many distant places. There is nothing on this earth, no adventure and no pleasure, that I have not tasted. Surely there must be some thrill left to experience," cried out Coyote into the wind.

Coyote swiftly traveled across the lands looking for what was missing from his life, whatever he had yet to complete. For years, Coyote walked across all the known lands in search of the thing that would suit his noble status. He traveled to the lands of the cold, white north and could find nothing to amuse him. He traveled the great plains but could find nothing to please him. He climbed over the mountain ranges but still could find nothing that would be worthy of the great Coyote.

After years of looking, Coyote decided to give up his search. "I must have experienced everything this world has to offer," he said, letting out a mournful howl at the stars in the sky. Hearing his sadness, a star fell from its place in the heavens and streaked across the darkness. One by one, the stars began to fall from the sky and put on the most beautiful dance. Coyote wanted to join the stars and dance in the night sky all across the world. It would be a pleasure fit for someone of his status.

The next night, Coyote returned to the same place and howled his sorrowful tune to the sky, entreating the stars to allow him to dance with them. He watched in amazement as the stars jumped across the black sky, dancing as they raced through the air. Coyote thought if he howled hard enough, he could get one of the stars to come close to him so that he might jump on it and fly with the star. Night after night, Coyote returned to the same spot and bellowed his music to the stars, asking if he might join in their dance. Coyote did this for three nights, and finally the brightest star in the night sky answered him.

"This is not a place for your kind, Coyote," said the star. "This is a world not like your own, and I am afraid that you cannot dance with us. You must remain in your place."

Staying in his place was something that Coyote was not very good at, and every night, he returned to the same spot and howled up into the sky, pleading for the stars to take him in their dance across the heavens. This went on for some time until the brightest star in the sky spoke again to Coyote.

"You have not listened to my warnings and have not stopped asking to dance with us. You leave me no choice but to grant your request and take you up into our world," said the bright star, which at once descended from the heavens. "Jump on from atop the nearest mountain."

Coyote at once climbed to the top of the highest mountain and tried to jump on the star as it zoomed by at full speed. But Coyote did not time his jump properly and only managed to take hold of the star's tail as it danced through the sky. Swept up into the black night, Coyote looked down upon the world from up high, and the earth began to move at an incredible speed beneath his feet.

He did his best to hold onto the star's tail as it flew about in the heavens, but the star's tail began to fade, and Coyote lost his grip. He tumbled out of the sky, and the star simply kept dancing through the night.

The bright star then said to him as he fell, "I warned you, Coyote, that this land was not for your kind. Your arrogance and self-importance blinded you, and now you will pay the price."

When Coyote came plunging down to the ground, his magical powers were knocked out of him, and he was condemned to live throughout the rest of existence as a common coyote, howling at the night sky in sorrow.

# The Eye Juggler

ONE BRIGHT MORNING AS Coyote walked through the forest, he heard the sound of two voices, laughing and singing:

> *Two go up,*
> *Two come down,*
> *Back in the head,*
> *Back in my crown.*

This, of course, made Coyote curious, so he followed the sound of the voices. Walking out of the forest, Coyote came upon two badgers, and one of them was throwing his eyes in the air and catching them with his head. Each time he did this, he would recite:

*Two go up,*
*Two come down,*
*Back in the head,*
*Back in my crown.*

And as he did this, the badger's friend would laugh with delight. Coyote also laughed out loud and startled the two badgers. They had never seen an animal like Coyote and ran off into the wood, fearful that the strange beast would eat them up.

"I own this magic. You cannot juggle your eyes better than I," Coyote called out to the badgers as they ran off into the distance. "I will show you how it is done."

Coyote then took out his eyes and tossed them up into the air and said:

*Two go up,*
*Two come down,*
*Back in the head,*
*Back in my crown.*

Coyote's eyes sailed high into the air, and as he said the words, his eyes landed back in their home. Even though the badgers were long gone, Coyote kept juggling his eyes and boasting of his incredible talents. Over and over again, Coyote threw his eyes into the air, reciting the same words so that his eyes might find their way home.

He tossed them behind his back, rolled them in his fingers and threw them into the clouds. But each time, Coyote recited the words, and his eyes would fall back into his head.

It just so happened that two ravens were flying by at the very moment that Coyote began to toss his eyes in the air, and they were curious to find out more about this crazy exercise that Coyote was doing. The two ravens landed on a nearby tree out of sight so they could devise a plan to fool Coyote.

The ravens had always been jealous of Coyote's strength of mind and body and secretly desired to remove the source of Coyote's power and take it for themselves. "We shall take his eyes to the sacred lands and try to uncover the source of his magic," said the ravens.

So the next time Coyote threw his eyes into the air, the two ravens swooped down and snatched them out of the air before Coyote could recite the words. In a flash, the ravens took his eyes and flew off into the distance, all the while laughing their evil laugh, "Caw, caw, caw…"

Blinded, Coyote tripped over rocks and smashed into trees as he tried to find his way around the forest. He knelt on the ground and felt like weeping, but he couldn't do that anymore.

He tried to follow the sound of the ravens' laughter, but they were too fast, and Coyote became completely lost. He wandered through the forest like a newborn pup on wobbly legs, stumbling and crashing into everything. Coyote moved on a little farther through the forest in this manner and was covered in cuts and bruises.

A young bluebird caught sight of the blind Coyote and could not help but feel sympathy for his plight. "Look," the young bluebird said to its mother. "Coyote is stumbling about. He is covered in bruises and only seeks assistance."

"Do not bother yourself with that beast, young one," said the bluebird mother. "His list of tricks is long, and that smile hides a row of sharp teeth supported by a lying tongue. Stay away from him. I have been around long enough to have seen many of his antics."

But like all young ones who do not take the council of their elders all the time, the young bluebird approached Coyote.

"Poor, blind creature," said the young bluebird, cautiously moving closer to Coyote. "Why do you wander about smacking into rocks and trees?"

"Well, hello, young one. I'm following the stars as they streak across the sky," said Coyote as he pointed to the sky. Can't you see them?" asked Coyote.

The young bluebird looked all about him but could not see the stars that Coyote was talking about. "I'm sorry, Coyote, but I don't see any star in the sky."

"What!" Coyote exclaimed. "How can you not, when they are right in front of you? I indeed have eyes, but they are very tiny. My eyes do not see well at short distances, but when I look into the sky, I can see all the wonders that the Great Spirit created. They are of such magnificence that you would not believe it if you did not witness it yourself. Come closer to me, and I will show you."

The young bluebird forgot about his mother's warning and stood right next to Coyote. The moment the young one was within reach, Coyote snatched him up, then pulled out the bluebird's eyes and threw them up in the air and said:

*Two go up,*
*Two come down,*
*Back in the head,*
*Back in my crown.*

The young bluebird's eyes now belonged to Coyote. "Foolish bird, when did you ever see stars with the sun high in the sky? You may be upset with me this day, but I have taught you a valuable lesson. Remember, just because someone says something is true does not mean they are right."

After Coyote had run off with the bluebird's eyes, the young one went to his mother. He told his mother how Coyote had tricked him and stolen his eyes.

"Did I not tell you to mind that Coyote? I will repair the damage, but next time, listen when I speak," said the bluebird's mother.

She took two blackberries and put them into his head, and they became his new eyes. That is why bluebirds' eyes are as black as night.

Coyote was happy to be able to see again, but the bluebird's eyes were far too small and did not fit into his head properly. Despite the fit, Coyote could now see, and he began to hunt for the two ravens who had stolen his sight.

After walking for two straight days through the forest with no sign of the ravens, Coyote suddenly heard a faint sound that was very familiar. As he got closer to the source, Coyote could clearly make out that it was the laughter of the two ravens who had stolen his eyes.

Sneaking through the forest in the direction of the noise, Coyote came upon the home of an old vulture woman. He saw the ancient vulture trying to warm her hands over a fire. Quickly recognizing that he could take advantage of her, Coyote hid his face under a hood and entered her house.

"Old woman, would you please allow a tired traveler to rest his feet by the fire for a little while?" asked Coyote.

"I do not get many visitors, but my nephews, two black-as-night ravens, recently stopped by," said the old vulture woman. "So it's nice to have people here."

"Are you afraid to live in the forest by yourself?" asked Coyote.

"I am afraid of nothing, except for Coyote," said the old woman, completely unaware of the danger that sat beside her. "I have been on this earth for a long time, and I know his tricks."

With one movement, Coyote threw off his disguise and grabbed the vulture woman in his jaws. Before he killed her, Coyote, said, "You don't know all my tricks old hag."

He then removed all her skin with his knife and then dressed himself in it. He looked almost like the old woman in every way except that he did not sound like her. Just then, the two ravens walked into the home and saw their aunt sitting by the fire. They were laughing as they walked into the room and sat down to warm their feet.

Coyote tried his best to mimic the voice of the old vulture woman. "What are you laughing at, boys?" he asked.

"Auntie, it was the funniest of things," said one raven. "We saw that stupid old Coyote throwing his eyes up into the air and then catching them. So when he threw them into the air once more, we stole them."

"My, Auntie, but your voice does not sound healthy," said the other raven. "Is everything all right?"

"Why, yes, child, everything is fine. I must have scratched my throat with a salmon bone," said the disguised Coyote. "What have you done with Coyote's eyes?"

"We took them down to the gathering place and danced around them so that we could try to learn of Coyote's powers," said one of the ravens. "We will take you, Auntie, and you shall join in the celebration."

Coyote was led out of the house and down to the gathering place where a great celebration was in full swing. All the creatures of the forest who had been tricked by Coyote were dancing around his eyes and singing victory songs.

This disrespect of Coyote's great eyes angered him, and he threw off the old vulture woman's skin and snatched up his eyes off the ground. He threw bluebird's tiny eyes into the woods, then tossed his own eyes in the air and said:

*Two go up,*
*Two come down,*
*Back in the head,*
*Back in my crown.*

Coyote's own eyes were now back where they belonged. As he ran from the gathering place, he called to the two ravens, "Maybe you should check on your auntie." He then disappeared into the woods, and he never again juggled his eyes.

As for the two ravens, they were looked down upon by the creatures of the forest and were forced to drag the skin of their aunt back to her home, where they found her body and brought her back to life. The two ravens told her what had happened and that Coyote had tricked her, so she beat them for not knowing better than to steal from someone like Coyote.

# The Strange Man

COYOTE TRAVELED ALONG the river and came to an area of calm running water where out in a canoe sat a man. Coyote stopped by the edge of the river just behind some bushes and watched the man as he fished. But this fishing was unlike any he had ever witnessed, for the man used his bare hands to pull up the mighty sturgeon.

Coyote thought this very curious behavior and continued to watch as the man dove deep into the water and did not surface for sometime before appearing with a large sturgeon held in both hands. The man then tossed the fish into the bottom of the boat, counted his catch and dove back under the water.

The moment the man disappeared below the surface, Coyote jumped into the river and swam to the stranger's canoe. He saw a load of fish on the bottom of the boat and took one up in his jaws, swimming back to shore with all haste to gobble up his prize. Hiding once again behind the cover of bushes, Coyote watched the strange man surface from the water with two giant sturgeons in each hand. The man tossed them into the canoe, climbed in and once again began to count his catch.

Coyote laughed as the man counted his fish. When he realized he had been robbed of a sturgeon, the man frantically began to search his boat and stared at the shoreline for any sign of the thief. The strange man held his finger in the air and pointed toward the sky, then to the water, then to the shore of the river. Coyote laughed harder at the man's misfortune, but he quieted himself when he saw the man's finger come to a stop, pointing exactly at the bush that Coyote was hiding behind. The man began paddling his canoe toward the shore. Coyote at once started a fire to cook and eat the fish before the man arrived, but he was not fast enough.

When the man came ashore, Coyote got a good look at the strange being for the first time and was shocked to see that the man had no mouth. His eyes, ears and nose were all in their proper places, but instead of a mouth, there was simply flesh. The man began to mumble strange noises, wave his arms about in a fuss and stare at Coyote in anger. Instead of being afraid, Coyote felt pity for the man with no mouth.

"Please sit with me, and we will cook your catch together and share the meat," said Coyote. He then lay the sturgeon down on a flat rock and cut it down its belly to remove the organs. Then he took a few stones and heated them up in the fire. Once they were hot, he put the stones inside the fish, cooking it from the inside out. Coyote then cut up the fish into little pieces and placed it in front of the man with no mouth.

Because he was not able to eat the fish, the man picked it up, sniffed it and then threw it into the woods. Upset, Coyote fetched the piece of sturgeon, brushed off the dirt and ate it himself.

"Foolish man. How can you waste good sturgeon!" said Coyote. But the man could not answer and only made a few mumbling noises that came out his nose. Coyote felt a deep sadness for the man as he had watched him smell the fish, never to taste its delicious meat. He stared carefully at the man's face and suddenly exclaimed, "I know! I shall make you a mouth that you can use to eat and to talk. You have allowed to me to have one of your sturgeon, therefore I will perform for you a kindness."

The man looked on in panic as Coyote took out his knife and came at him. The man tried to dodge Coyote's attempt to slash him, but he was too slow, and the blade caught him right across the face, releasing a torrent of blood. Through the blood, the man opened his mouth for the first time and took a deep breath.

"Go wash your mouth in the river," instructed Coyote.

When the man returned from the river, his mouth was completely healed, and he spoke for the first time. "Thank you, Coyote. At first I was going to kill you for taking my fish. You are welcome to have my entire catch if you might help me further," he said. "My entire village is afflicted with the same problem. One day we were visited by an evil spirit, and it was he who removed our mouths and covered them over with flesh. We have been suffering ever since, and my people are at the point of starvation."

Coyote traveled to the village and cut open the mouths of all the villagers. They used their new freedom to thank Coyote and prepared a large feast in his honor so that they might taste food once again. The people wanted to make Coyote their chief, but he insisted that he had to leave, and the next morning, they woke to find that Coyote was gone.

# Coyote and Leech Woman

COYOTE WAS TIRED, HUNGRY and frustrated after days of trying to find a salmon to eat. He walked for a long time along the mighty river and still could find nothing to eat. He finally returned to his home to rest for the night.

"I wish I had some salmon to eat," he said out loud. Coyote then went to sleep, and in the morning when he opened the door to his house, he found two fresh salmon lying at his feet. Coyote picked up the salmon and looked all around him for the person who had given him this gift.

"Hello," he called out, but no answer came. Fearing that whomever had left the salmon would come back for them, Coyote started a fire and ate the salmon.

The next day, Coyote woke up and decided to try his luck again at finding fish, but after three days out on the water, Coyote gave up all hope of finding the elusive salmon.

"What does this person know that I don't when it comes to fishing? I have been hunting these waters since the salmon first spawned," thought Coyote. "I wish I had some salmon to eat, for I haven't eaten in days."

Coyote went to bed hungry that night, but when he woke up the next morning, he found two more salmon waiting by his front door. "The fish cannot be hearing my calls and walking to my door. Someone must be leaving them for me to eat. I will stay up tonight and watch for my mysterious sponsor," said Coyote. That night, when he went to bed, Coyote again wished for some salmon to eat and waited for his benefactor to arrive. Late into the night, he stood behind his door, staring out of a small knothole, watching for the salmon fisherman. Coyote was just about to fall asleep when he saw his neighbor coming out of the woods. He could not mistake her flat body and gnarled teeth. She was Leech Woman, and she had never had a husband.

Coyote burst out of the door and startled Leech Woman, who dropped her fish and ran off into the forest. "That's right, you had better run, you hideous woman. I'd recognize your flat, slimy body in any light. I had hoped that it was going to be a beautiful virgin maiden who favored me with gifts, but instead I find your wrinkly face."

Although she looked like a monster, Leech Woman was very sensitive about her appearance and became angry over Coyote's rude remarks. Although ugly, she was a woman of great respect, for it was she who controlled all the salmon in the waters. But she had fallen in love with Coyote and took his words to heart.

Coyote picked up the salmon that Leech Woman had dropped and returned to his house to devour his prize. After he finished eating, Coyote realized that he might not get to eat salmon again unless he made amends with his neighbor.

Coyote walked over to Leech Woman's home and entered her front door. She was sitting in the corner and did not pay him any attention. He spoke sweet words to her and promised a thousand kindnesses, but she still would not acknowledge his presence. This angered Coyote greatly, so he hit her with one of his clubs and knocked her out.

"That's what happens when you do not answer when spoken to," said Coyote, placing her limp body in the corner. Coyote then dressed in her robes and looked very much like Leech Woman. Walking out to the edge of the river, Coyote called out to the salmon, and suddenly, hundreds of the fish swam before him. But the salmon were suspicious of this Leech Woman because she normally never called them out in the mid-afternoon sun. Looking at their queen a little closer, one salmon noticed something different about her. "This is not our queen. Look at those slanted eyes and long nose. It's Coyote!"

Because Coyote had been discovered, Leech Woman's clothes began to fall from his body, and the salmon carried them away downstream. Coyote had lost, and he returned home with nothing to eat.

# The Pangs of Hunger

ONE DAY, WHILE WALKING along the edge of the Columbia River, Coyote's stomach was in need of food. But it was not the time of the salmon run, and food fit for a Coyote was nowhere to be found. During his journey, all he had were a few meager berries and a handful of bitter roots to eat. "This is no way to live for someone as important as myself," he thought.

Wandering along in such a manner, Coyote happened upon Buffalo, who looked fat and well fed. "Hello, friend. I am Coyote. I have been wandering these lands for some time and have not had much to eat other than a few berries. I see that you are big and strong. Could you turn me into a buffalo so that I, too, need not starve?" asked Coyote.

Buffalo did not acknowledge Coyote's presence and continued to graze on the lush, green grasses along the riverside. But Coyote was never one to back down from a challenge and repeated his request, "Turn me into a buffalo so I will stay fat and not go hungry." Coyote continued to say this throughout the day until it became so irritating to Buffalo that he finally agreed to the request.

"Foolish Coyote, I will grant your wish, but to become a buffalo, you must have great courage and even greater trust in other buffalo. I believe that you do not possess these traits to pass the first test in becoming a member of our tribe," said Buffalo.

"How do you know my character? I can take anything you can deliver," boasted Coyote.

"If you think you are so brave, Coyote," smirked Buffalo, "this is what you will have to do. You will go to the center of that field, lie down in the grass and remain absolutely still. I will then charge at you with all my strength, and I will toss you in the air with my powerful horns."

"That's it?" replied a confident Coyote.

Coyote sauntered over to the field and lay down in the thick grass. Once Coyote was positioned in the grass, Buffalo worked himself into an incredible rage. The ground began to tremble under the power of his hooves, and his grunting could be heard in the neighboring valleys. He tore up the earth, hot air poured from his nostrils, and his eyes, burning with anger, turned toward Coyote and stared deep into his soul.

Coyote's heart welled up with fear as Buffalo began his charge. "Surely this is just a test and Buffalo will not actually toss me into the air with his massive horns," he thought. But Buffalo showed no signs of stopping his charge. The pressure became too much for Coyote to handle, and in the final moment before he was to be thrown into the air, he jumped out of the way.

"I knew you could not handle the pressure. You do not have the courage and sense of trust to be part of our tribe," scolded Buffalo.

Turning his back to Coyote, Buffalo resumed grazing on the rich grasses.

"Please, let me try again," pleaded Coyote. "I promise I will not move a muscle."

Coyote begged and pleaded with Buffalo until he finally relented.

"I will do this only once more. I warn you, Coyote, do not move a muscle, and you shall get your wish."

Once more, Buffalo worked himself into a frenzy, stomping on the ground and breathing steam out through his nose. Coyote found his spot on the field and held firm. This time, he resolved to not move.

Buffalo charged, and Coyote felt his horns in his rib cage as he was sent flying into the air. When he came down and hit the ground, he suddenly changed into a buffalo. Coyote/Buffalo could not believe the sudden transformation and immediately thanked Buffalo for helping him. "Now I will never go hungry and will live off my fat during the winter. Thank you so much, wise Buffalo."

But Buffalo did not hear the words. He simply returned to feed on the grass.

Wanting to test out his new body and all the things it could do, Coyote/Buffalo set out on his own and began tasting all the various items that Buffalo eat—all the grass, bushes and other verdure he could find. At first, Coyote/Buffalo did not understand why the buffalo would eat such things as grass when tasty salmon were in the river, but the more grasses and leaves he tried, the more he began to enjoy their fibrous flavor. He was slowly losing his Coyote tastes and was becoming more like Buffalo by the moment. He felt big and strong, and, most importantly, his belly was never empty. He felt like the king of all living creatures; no longer did he have to sneak and slink through life or beg for food.

As Coyote/Buffalo looked across the expansive valley, with his horns held high toward the sun, he saw something approach him from off in the distance. It was his brother, Fox.

"I know it is you, Coyote. You might be in the form of a buffalo, but you still have the shifty eyes of Coyote," said Fox. "You are so fat and filled with strength! How was this done? I want to be free and fat like you. Tell me how you managed to become a buffalo," begged Fox.

But Coyote/Buffalo did not respond. He simply turned his back and continued to feed on the green grass.

"Please, Brother, do not condemn me to a life of scavenging and starvation. You must change me into a buffalo," pleaded Fox over and over again. He kept repeating himself so often that finally Coyote/Buffalo gave in to the pressure.

"Calm yourself, Fox," said Coyote. "I will change you into a buffalo. But you must possess the strength of courage and trust that all buffalo have. Only then can you become part of our tribe," said Coyote/Buffalo.

"I have more than enough courage and strength of character to be two buffalo. What must I do?" asked Fox.

"Lie down in the field, and I will charge at you. You cannot move a muscle, or the magic will not work. I will then knock you into the air, and you will be changed into a buffalo."

Fox sat among the green grass and watched as Coyote/Buffalo worked up a terrific rage just as Buffalo had done. He stomped on the ground, shaking the earth beneath his mighty hooves. He lashed out in the air with his powerful horns, sending a chill through Fox's body. Coyote/Buffalo began his charge and set his sights on Fox. Despite the danger to his life, Fox did not move or even flinch. Coyote/Buffalo hit Fox with such force that they both flew up into the air, and when they came down, Fox remained the same, but Coyote/Buffalo was transformed into just Coyote again.

"Ah, what kind of magic is this? What have you done to me, Fox?" accused Coyote. "I am no longer fat and healthy."

"This was not my doing," replied Fox. "You were given this gift by a very powerful buffalo, but his gifts are unique to him. You tried to imitate his magic and failed, so you have returned to your true form."

Coyote chased his brother across the valley but could not match the speed and agility of Fox. Dejected at being returned to his original form,

Coyote tried to mimic the buffalo by eating some grass but found that it was not to his taste.

"How does Buffalo stay so fat on this grass? I much prefer the taste of a fat salmon," said Coyote, as he walked along the river and through the forests looking for his next meal.

# The Spirits of
# the Sun and Moon

COYOTE WOULD OFTEN GO away on long hunting trips, leaving his wife at home with their two children. She was grateful to have her two kids because all their other children had grown up and left home to start families of their own. For many months at a time, while Coyote followed the herds, it was just her and their two little boys.

Every morning when the sun rose, Coyote's wife looked beside her and felt very lonely. She spent her days watching over her children as they grew into fine young men. One boy was named White Spirit because his skin was the color of milk, and the other was named Red Fire because his skin was red like the sun. The boys were her only companions.

Days turned into months and months into years, and still Coyote did not return. His wife feared that he might have been killed. But one bright, sunny day, Coyote returned from the long hunt, and the family celebrated with a big feast. Coyote was glad to see that his boys had grown into strong young men, but he could see that they needed some time with their father.

Every morning, Coyote woke his sons up and took them out into the wilderness. He put them through rigorous exercises and tests of strength and endurance to try to break their wills, all in an effort to turn them into great warriors. After many moons of training, Coyote's sons had become the mightiest of all warriors.

Coyote heard from a neighbor that a grand council meeting was planned to decide who would become the new spirits of the sun and the moon. The sun and moon spirits had killed each other over who should control the sky, and now neither the sun nor the moon rose in the heavens. When Coyote informed his sons, they immediately wanted to go to the council. Once again, Coyote left his poor wife at home while he took his sons on a trip that lasted seven days.

When Coyote and his sons arrived at the council, they found the people in great distress. It had been many days with no sun or moon in the sky, and there was a fear that everything on earth would simply perish because all life was subject to the rhythms of the sun and the moon. The council had tried to find two people worthy of taking the positions of the sky spirits, but all had failed.

Coyote stepped forward and offered to become the spirit of the sun. He then appeared for the first time in the sky above and was doing an excellent job at warming the earth, but he could not resist spying on the people below him. From his perch in the sky, he would call down to people as they made love or flirted with someone who wasn't their spouse. The people grew angry at the eyes watching them from above and protested that Coyote was allowed to take such an important job. Coyote then descended from the sky and offered his sons for the job.

"But, Father, we wish to stay here on earth. Mother is very lonely, and we wish to remain here to take care of her," said Coyote's son White Spirit.

Everyone on the council was very disappointed by the sons' refusal to become the spirits in the sky, all except one. At the council was Frog Woman, and she had fallen in love with White Spirit. She wanted him for a husband and was determined to have him one way or another.

"White Spirit, please take this drink, for I know you are thirsty after your long trip away from home," said Frog Woman, handing him a drink she had just drugged.

White Spirit fell into a deep sleep, and when he woke up, he was in the lodge of the Frog Woman, and every part of his body was paralyzed except for his head. Frog Woman then took off her robes and made love to White Spirit.

"You have now become my husband," she told him.

But White Spirit did not want to be with Frog Woman because she was one of the ugliest women he had ever seen.

"I refuse to be forced into marriage. You have poisoned me and made me your husband against my will. I will never love you," said White Spirit.

Hearing these words greatly angered Frog Woman, and she jumped onto White Spirit's face. After some time, the poison finally wore off White Spirit, and he did everything he could to pull Frog Woman off his face, but she would not budge. She just stuck to his face, croaking a sad tune. White Spirit left the home with Frog Woman still attached to his face and sought the help of his father.

"Please help me, Father. Frog Woman captured me and professed her love to me, and when I did not return it, she jumped on my face and will not let go," said White Spirit.

Coyote and White Spirit tried everything they could think of to get the slimy creature from White Spirit's face. They tried using fire and magic powders as well as brute strength, but nothing they did removed her from his face. White Spirit was so ashamed of the way he looked that he agreed to become the spirit of the moon. That way, no one could see how ugly he had become. Red Fire would not leave his brother's side and decided to become the spirit of the sun.

"Brother, though you are disfigured, you will not have to live out eternity alone. I will become the spirit of the sun and shine brightly through the day. You will take the night sky so that everyone will be asleep and not have to look upon that horrible Frog Woman on your face," said Red Spirit.

To this day, the brothers remain in the sky, and at night, if you look up at the moon, the dark spots you see are those of Frog Woman, who is still stubbornly attached to the face of the man she loves. White Spirit's brother still keeps him company in the sky kingdom and comes out every day to shine down on the people.

# The Cheating Wife

LONG BEFORE HUMANS EXISTED on earth, Wolf lived in harmony with his beautiful wife. Every day, he went hunting and would return with plenty of food as well as fine pelts for her to sew into clothing. Nature provided everything they needed, and they were very much in love.

But one day, when Wolf returned from a hunt, his wife said that she did not love him anymore. It was a hard thing for Wolf to accept, for he was a proud man and did not want to let her go. She agreed to stay with Wolf, but things only got worse for the pair. When Wolf returned from one of his hunts, he noticed that his wife had changed. It had become so bad that she spurned his advances.

Wolf could not understand what was going on with his wife.

It happened one day that Wolf's brother, Coyote, came to visit. They had not been together long before Coyote noticed something different in his sister-in-law's behavior. She did not look either of them in the eye and did not speak much, if at all. Coyote was immediately suspicious that she might be in love with another. But not having any proof, Coyote could not go to his brother without knowing for sure that this was the problem. He decided to follow her as she went about her daily chores to see how she spent her time while her husband was out on the hunt.

For days, Coyote followed Wolf's wife around the forest while she picked berries, tended to her garden and went down to the river to fetch water. Coyote could not see anything suspicious about her behavior, until one day when he noticed that every time that she went to the river, she would sit on the bank and quietly whisper into the deep waters. Coyote could not figure out what she was saying so he disguised himself as a little bird and flew close enough to hear her singing the most beautiful of songs.

> *Every day he comes to me*
> *From so far along.*
> *Every day I know he thinks of me*

*He can do no wrong.*
*Every day he whispers to me,*
*"How I love you so."*
*Every day I know he will*
*Never let me go.*

As Coyote sat in the tree still disguised as a little bird, he watched as the river suddenly swelled and a great wave of water pushed up the river-banks. He could hardly believe his little bird eyes when he saw a great whale emerge from the depths of the river. The moment it touched land, the great whale changed into a very handsome man. Coyote could do nothing as the man made love to his brother's wife. Infuriated, Coyote flew back to his brother's house and transformed back into his normal form. Coyote searched for his brother and found him out collecting firewood.

"Brother, I have some bad news," Coyote said. "I have seen your wife with another man, and they have bonded their love. I did not want this to be true, so I followed her and confirmed that she is in love with a great whale. But I think that she is under a magic spell and does not know the consequences of her actions. Come with me now and we shall stop this."

The two brothers ran down to the river's edge where Coyote said the couple would be, but they only found a piece of her clothing. They knew at once that Wolf's wife had been kidnapped and taken to the world of the water tribe. Wolf was overcome with vicious anger, and he vowed to do anything to get his wife back from the water's depths.

Coyote and Wolf went to the water's edge every day but could find no way to rescue Wolf's wife from the water monster's grasp. They howled at the moon in sorrow for their lost family member. It was then that the light of the moon revealed two young maidens sitting on the surface of the water. Together they sang:

*We have come!*
 *We have come!*
*To your surface we*
 *were led*
*By our master, who*
 *searches for*
*Some food for his*
 *wife to be fed.*
*Oh tragic, is his life*
*Oh tragic, they*
 *would say*
*If master were to*
 *lose this wife*
*Like the other one*
 *yesterday.*

*We have come!*
 *We have come!*
*To your surface we*
 *were led*
*By our master, who*
 *searches for*
*Some food for his*
 *wife to be fed.*
*Oh tragic, is his life*
*Oh tragic, they*
 *would say*
*If master were to*
 *lose this wife*
*Like the other one*
 *yesterday.*

The maidens from the land of water then walked ashore and began to gather food for the great whale's prisoner. They gathered berries, pulled up roots and even stole some dried meat from Wolf's home. Wolf jumped into the house and blocked the exit. The two maidens screamed, but they could not fight off the angry Wolf spirit. Wolf grabbed them by their throats and demanded to know where the monster held his beloved. The maidens obeyed Wolf's demands and told him that the great whale kept his bride underneath the waves of the Big Falls along the mighty river's path. Together the water maidens called:

*Beware! Beware!*
   *Heed our call,*
*Our master is evil,*
*Our master cannot*
   *fall.*
*He rules with anger*
   *like no other*
*And will swiftly kill*
*Anyone who tries*
   *to take his lover.*

*Beware! Beware!*
   *Heed our call,*
*Our master is evil,*
*Our master cannot*
   *fall.*
*He rules with anger*
   *like no other*
*And will swiftly kill*
*Anyone who tries*
   *to take his lover.*

But Wolf did not pay any attention to their warnings. Wolf and Coyote traveled to the Big Falls and looked down into the water. Just beneath its surface, they saw a world like no other, with everything blue and green in color. It was a world in which Wolf and Coyote did not belong, so they killed two frogs and dressed in their skins. As frogs live in water and on land, Wolf and Coyote would be protected from drowning as long as they wore the frog skins.

Jumping into the water with a great splash, Coyote and Wolf entered the strange world. They passed by the water people without attracting too much attention, with only an odd look or two from the elders of the water folk. Walking through the village, they spotted a grandiose house that they were sure must belong to the arrogant whale.

Walking through the doorway of the great whale's home, Wolf and Coyote saw Wolf's stolen wife sitting side by side with the thief. Still in disguise, Coyote and Wolf presented a bag of berries and dried meat to the great whale.

"The water maidens have failed you, master of these waters," said Wolf. "Take this food for your new wife." Wolf handed over the food to his stolen wife, and she happily ate it all up.

"Thank you, kind frogs. I was worried that I might lose another wife because the people from the world above eat strange things. For your help, you can stay the night in my home," said the great whale.

Coyote and Wolf waited that night for everyone to fall asleep. Then, when all was still, they walked up to the sleeping whale and cut off his head. With his head removed, the great whale's power over Wolf's wife faded, and she suddenly came back to her senses.

"My dear husband, thank you for saving me from this monster. Please take me back to our home," she whispered to her beloved.

Coyote, Wolf and the stolen wife quietly spirited away under the cover of night, taking with them the monster's head as a prize. In the morning, the people of the water woke to find the great whale had been killed and that his stolen wife had been taken.

The great whale had been a tyrant, forcing the people to work for him and making their lives miserable. For the water people, his death was a good omen, so they celebrated by dancing around his body for days and used his blubber to light their fires.

Wolf and Coyote wanted to make sure that the great whale never returned to the fresh waters of the Interior, so they cast his head toward the setting sun and it landed in the vast saltwater seas.

"Never again shall you be able to return to these waters, monster," said Coyote. "You are a prisoner of the salt waters and can never again steal the wives of men and take them as prisoners."

The great whale's body became whole again when the monster's head hit the cool waters, and he cursed the people of the land for what they had done to him.

# Coyote in Lust

ONE HOT SUMMER DAY, Coyote was wandering along the river when he heard the sounds of five young maidens frolicking in the waters by the river's edge. They were five of the most beautiful women Coyote had ever seen, and a sudden wave of heat passed through his body. He had to have his way with those women.

"I want to have fun with all of the women, but if one were to recognize me, my game would be over," thought Coyote. For his trick to work, he would have to disguise his true identity. Coyote believed that women always fall in love when they see a baby, so he transformed himself into a cute baby boy and launched himself down the river on a raft made of driftwood.

It wasn't long before the raft passed in front of the first beautiful young maiden. Letting out a cry of distress when she saw the infant, she pulled him from the water.

"Oh, poor creature. Let me take you to the shore and get you something to eat," she said. When they reached the shore and were out of sight of the other maidens, Coyote changed into the form of a handsome man and had his way with the first maiden. He then changed himself into a baby again and drifted farther down the river to the next maiden. Once she spotted the child in the water, her heart opened up.

"How could someone lose such a precious package," she said as she tickled the baby's cheeks. But again, the moment they were out of sight, Coyote changed into a man and had his way with the beautiful young maiden. Coyote then fooled two other of the young maidens in the exact same manner before coming to the fifth, the youngest and most beautiful of the maidens. Coyote looked lustfully at her soft skin, full lips and ample breasts and knew he had to have her. But in the rush to satisfy his desire, Coyote forgot to transform every part of himself into a baby.

The youngest maiden noticed the baby floating down the river, and she knew immediately that something was not right. "The child looks a little different. I must get a closer look to see what is wrong," she said. So she grabbed the baby from the water, put him on the riverbank and unlaced his clothing. "In all my days I have never seen such a baby!" she screamed. "This is surely Coyote."

In his haste to transform into the baby, Coyote forgot to change the one part of himself that could not be mistaken for a baby's. When the maiden saw Coyote's member sticking straight in the air, she tossed him back into the river. Coyote thought he was smart, but he was not careful enough.

# Saving the Salmon

ONE DAY, AS COYOTE WALKED through the forest, he was told by a passing bluebird that two old sisters had trapped all the fish in the mighty Columbia River and that the people might soon starve if the fish were not returned to the waters.

Coyote loved fish, especially salmon, and he vowed to help the people and free the creatures of the river from the old hags' prison. The bluebird had told Coyote that the old sisters had trapped all the creatures in a large pond that led from the river.

So Coyote departed, and a few days later, he came to the spot by the river that the bluebird had told him about. Coyote quickly jumped into the reeds by the water when the two old hags appeared along the bank with nets to trap more fish. Beyond the old women, he could see the gate that held the fish in their prison. To get to the gate, he would have to walk past the two women. Coyote needed a disguise, so he fashioned a basket out of the reeds and the bark of a tree and transformed himself into a baby boy. He then jumped into the basket and threw himself to the mercy of the river, sending the basket tumbling through the dangerous waters.

Hearing the cries of the frightened baby, the two old women caught the basket in their nets. "Surely someone upriver must have lost this boy in a storm," said the eldest sister. "A boy is better than a fish."

They took the baby from its basket and carried it back to their pond, where they had a large house. The younger sister looked upon the baby with a curious eye. "Elder sister, do you not think this baby is odd. I think it might be Coyote come to trick us."

"Don't be stupid, younger sister. I have been around on this earth longer than you, so I know the trickster when I see him," said the eldest with certainty. "Now let us return home and find something to feed this child."

So the two women took the baby into their house and settled him into a crib. The eldest then went into the pond, pulled out a salmon, cooked it over the fire and gave some to the baby. Coyote ate everything in one mouthful.

"Why, this is a hungry child," said the eldest. "Sister, please fetch me another salmon so that I might feed this boy again. It would seem he has a great appetite for fish."

Coyote watched as the younger sister retrieved the fish from the pond by lifting a large gate and then selecting a salmon. He thought that if he could get to the gate, the salmon could escape into the great river. But the women fed Coyote so much fish that he became very sleepy and napped for several hours.

The women took the opportunity to return to their fishing by the river and left Coyote alone. When Coyote awoke, he transformed himself back into his normal form and walked to the large gate by the pond. He tried to lift the gate to release the fish, but the gate was under a spell and weighed too much for him to manage. So Coyote transformed into a mighty grizzly bear and lifted the gate high into the air. A sudden torrent of water rushed out of the pond, and all the fish from the river spilled back into the Columbia and headed upstream.

When the two old women saw all the fish swimming past them in the river, they ran back to their pond and saw the destruction of their prison caused by Coyote.

"I knew it was that evil Coyote, Sister," said the youngest. "He has taken all our food and destroyed our work."

Coyote changed back into his original form and confronted the two old sisters. "Your greed has led you to steal the fish from the people. They sit and starve in their villages while you gorge babies and yourselves. Shame on you, old sisters," said Coyote. "The fish is for the people that will inherit this land."

The two sisters tried to plead their case, but Coyote was too furious at their greed to hear their words. "You will become common swallows. You will never again get to taste the flesh of fish, for your have eaten your share. From now on, you will eat insects and use your mouth to catch them in the air. This will be your food, and you can only watch as the people below fish this mighty river."

Coyote willed the women to change into swallows. The two old sisters flew up into the evening sky and began eating up the flies and mosquitoes. The taste was bitter in their mouths, and they screamed their disgust as they flew overhead. Thus did Coyote create the swallow and give the fish back to the people.

# The Tribe of Flies

LONG AGO, THE FLY PEOPLE were the first to perform the sun dance. It was a secret they guarded jealously, and they killed anyone who inquired about it. The sun dance was a powerful tool for the Fly people—it gave them their energy and cured their ailments. The sun dance made them very strong, and many went in search of its secrets, but none ever returned from their travels.

It was said that no one ever returned from the Flies' lands because the crawlers hatched out of their eggs and consumed the Fly people's victims. It was a secret that was well kept for generations, until the day Coyote heard of the Fly people's sun dance and wanted that power for himself.

He had been warned not to pursue the secret, but Coyote was stubborn, and his curiosity would not let him leave it alone.

Coyote traveled to the land of the Fly people during the time of the sun dance and disguised himself as one of them to gain entry into their village. The disguise seemed to work at first, as all the Fly people gathered in the center of the village and began to perform the intricate dance in praise of the sun. Coyote tried to keep up with the Fly people, but he had never performed such a dance and struggled to follow along. The Fly people knew at once that an intruder was among them and was trying to steal their dance. The chief of the Fly people pointed to Coyote.

"People, we have an imposter among us, and he is trying to steal our dance," proclaimed the chief, bringing the sun dance to a sudden halt. The Fly people surrounded Coyote and ripped off his disguise.

"Coyote, I should have guessed it was you," said the Fly chief.

"Why will you not share your power?" asked Coyote.

"It was given to us alone, and we need the power to survive. You shall not leave here alive," said the Fly chief, who then cast thousands of eggs onto

Coyote, covering his body in a slimy, white swarm. The eggs began to hatch, and the white crawlers emerged. They at once attacked Coyote with their massive teeth and began to devour him. In just a matter of minutes, Coyote was completely stripped of his flesh. The Fly people took Coyote's bones and threw them just outside their village.

Coyote's brother, Fox, was traveling in the area and happened upon the bones. He jumped over them three times, and Coyote came back to life. Angry at having been denied his prize, Coyote resolved to find someone to help him steal the secret of the sun dance so that he could enact his revenge on the Fly people for killing him.

Coyote searched for someone who could survive an attack from the Fly people. He traveled to the home of Beaver and asked if he would help him discover the secret of the sun dance.

"Coyote, you must not have regained all of your brain! I have heard the stories of the vicious Fly people and the appetite of their young crawlers," said Beaver. "Look at me, Coyote. I am plump and slow. How would I fare in a fight that you yourself lost so miserably? Now please leave me. I have a dam to build before winter arrives."

Coyote then traveled to the home of Frog Woman. He told her about his experience with the Fly people and the power of the secrets they kept. Coyote knew that Frog Woman desired to have power as much as he did, and he was sure she would help him.

"But I can't go, for I am unable to dance. I have been cursed with webbed feet, and although I am one of the finest swimmers among all the peoples, my feet just cannot find a rhythm. I am afraid this quest is your own," replied Frog Woman.

Coyote left the home of Frog Woman, angry at not having found any help, but then Coyote thought of Snake. He knew Snake to be a very vicious character who could kill beasts with a single strike from his fangs. Snake at the time had many legs and was known as a dancer. Coyote traveled to the house of Snake and told him of his plans.

"I like the sound of your plan, Coyote, and I will take the power of the sun dance away from the Fly people for our benefit," hissed Snake.

So Snake traveled with Coyote to the village of the Fly people. When they arrived, Snake walked into the dance and tried to copy the Fly people. Immediately, the chief called out the intruder and threw hundreds of eggs upon Snake. At once, the pulsating crawlers emerged and sank their jaws all along Snake's back. But the crawlers' jaws could not pierce the scales that protected almost all of Snake's body. Snake, however, in his arrogance and temper, forgot that his legs were left unprotected from the bites, and within minutes, the crawlers had eaten Snake's legs. This is why snakes crawl along the ground on their stomachs.

Coyote left the lands of the Fly people again in anger and could not figure out a way to get the power of the sun dance. He decided to give up and began the long walk back to his home.

Defeat, however, was not something Coyote accepted easily, and all along his path through the forests, he cursed his fate and that of the Fly people for what they had done to him.

"Would you please be quiet!" screamed a voice.

Coyote turned in the direction of the sound and saw Porcupine lying down in the branches of a tree.

"Everyone in the forest knows that you have been humiliated by the Fly people. Why do you not just leave it alone?" exclaimed Porcupine.

"You wouldn't be so calm and comfortable there in your tree if you had been eaten by those things. The Fly people viciously hide the secret of the sun dance and will not share their powers," wailed Coyote like a child who had lost his toy. On and on Coyote complained into the day and howled his sorrowful song at night.

Porcupine tried everything he could do to block out Coyote's wails, but nothing worked. Coyote's lamenting cries went on and on, echoing through the forest for days until Porcupine had had enough.

"Coyote, this must stop now. I will help you under one condition. You must immediately stop your wailing and leave these once-peaceful forests," scolded Porcupine.

Coyote naturally agreed to the terms and departed at once with his new partner for the village of the Fly people. Upon arriving, Coyote sent Porcupine into the center of the village where the Fly people had gathered and were performing their sun dance. Coyote would watch and learn the dance from afar. Porcupine walked among the Fly people and began to dance. He was instantly discovered by the chief and covered in the white eggs of their children.

Coyote turned his head so as not to witness the carnage that was about to be unleashed on Porcupine. But when the crawlers erupted from their pulsating egg sacks, they received a rough welcome from the sharp quills of Porcupine. Every time a crawler lunged forward to bite him, it became impaled on Porcupine's spikes and died. The Fly people were not known for their intelligence, however, and continued to attack Porcupine. He ended up killing all but a few of the smallest of the Fly people.

"From this day forward, the Fly people will no longer be able to kill or eat the flesh of others. They will feed off the vilest substances on the planets, the excrement of beasts will be their dinner table, and they must bury their offspring in the rotting meat of corpses," pronounced Porcupine.

Watching from a distance, Coyote was able to figure out the steps of the sun dance and forever removed that source of power from the Fly people. And that is why today, the people have the sun dance. Coyote stole it from the Flies with the help of Porcupine and shared it with the people when they came to earth.

# The Hungry Woman and the Great River Rock

ONCE LONG AGO ON THE banks of the mighty Fraser River, the salmon did not pass the villages that awaited their yearly return. The winter had been one of the worst in recent memory, and the supplies of dried meat had all but run out.

In order to survive, the people had come to rely on the annual run of the salmon, but this summer, the fishermen returned to their villages with nothing but the nets they had left with. The only food the people had for their children were a few tiny berries and bitter roots that had yet to mature. The people waited for weeks by the edge of the river for the salmon to return, but the river remained empty. The best hunters were sent out into the forests to hunt for bigger game, but they returned with just a few rodents, not nearly enough to feed a village. Soon the people began to suffer for want of food, and desperation set in among the villages along the river.

A woman in one of the villages had three children and no food to feed them. Ka-eel's husband had left the village for the mountains to hunt for anything he could find and had not yet returned, leaving Ka-eel to provide for her children. Every night, her children cried themselves to sleep for want of food. Her situation, like that of the rest of the people, had become desperate.

Unable to sit idly by while her children starved to death, Ka-eel took a net down to the river to see if she could catch a salmon. She knew there was little hope of finding one, but she had to try. For several days, she swept the river with her net but continued to come up empty. Reports passed through the village farther down the river that no salmon had been seen, but still she cast her net through the waters, praying that she would catch a salmon for her children.

Then, one early morning as she swept the river, she felt something in her net—she had caught a salmon. She quickly pulled the fish from the river, wrapped it in leaves and bark and hid it in the forest to retrieve later. She knew that she was breaking the ancient traditions of her tribe when catching the first salmon of the season, but if she did nothing, her children would surely die. Tradition stated that the first salmon must be honored in ceremony, or the spirits would be angered at the lack of respect. But the cries of Ka-eel's hungry children outweighed the requirements of tradition.

When darkness fell across the land, Ka-eel retrieved the salmon and took it home to her children. They all ate their fill of the delicious pink flesh, but the moment Ka-eel and her children finished the last bits of salmon, the skies suddenly turned dark. Great black clouds rolled in off the mountains, a fierce wind whipped along the path of the river and the fury of the thunder spirit poured down from above. The elders of the village gathered in council and knew that someone must have done something to anger the spirits.

The medicine man, whose knowledge of the spirit world was the greatest among his people, tried to appease the spirits by chanting songs and praying to the world above, but it only served to make matters worse. The wind began to bend the tree branches, lightning issued forth from the clouds and a torrential rain poured down on the beleaguered faces of the people.

Ka-eel watched all the commotion from her lodge, hoping that the spirits would calm their fury over her insults.

"Oh, Great Spirit, please calm your fury, for I had to do something to save my children," said Ka-eel, looking up into the dark clouds. But her pleas went unheard, and the storm grew more violent. The wind then pulled Ka-eel from her lodge and carried her high into the air. She tried to free herself, but the strength of the wind held her within its tight grip. The villagers watched in horror as Ka-eel was lifted into the sky and tossed about like a child's toy. The wind then carried her out over the river. She was held a few feet above the water as a torrent raged below.

Then, as suddenly as the storm had begun, it died off, dropping Ka-eel into the waters beneath her. She struggled for a moment against the force of the river, but the waves soon washed over her, and Ka-eel sunk into the depths. The villagers watched all of this unfold from the shores, as no one was willing to tamper with the will of an angry spirit. As they watched the spot where Ka-eel had disappeared, the waters suddenly began to boil.

Something great in size was trying to push its way through to the surface, but in the crashing of the white water, the people could not tell if it was Ka-eel fighting off the spirits or some other danger sent to punish the entire village. The people slowly backed away from the river and saw a giant boulder emerge from the depths where Ka-eel had been dropped. The people could not figure out what had happened and called upon the spirit of Coyote to explain. Coyote suddenly appeared before the people.

"You have called me here to explain what has just occurred," said Coyote. "The woman, Ka-eel, caught the first salmon of the season, but instead of following the tradition of prayers to the spirits with the rest of the village, she greedily took the fish home and fed her family alone. This is a grave offense to the spirits of the salmon and the river, and a price had to be paid. Ka-eel now sits in the center of the river, changed into the giant boulder, and for all of eternity, she will watch over the salmon as they make their way up the river."

The news of Ka-eel's fate was carried on the wind into the mountains where it reached the ears of her husband, who had remained in the forests on the hunt. Hearing the fate of his wife, Ka-eel's husband wept. He cried so many tears that they turned into the small rivers and streams that run down from the mountains into the mighty Fraser River to this day.

# Coyote and his Beautiful Daughter

LONG AGO, COYOTE AND HIS daughter lived together. Coyote once had a wife, but she was killed, and he was left to take care of his daughter alone. The loss of his wife had affected Coyote greatly, leaving him sickly and ill. It was left to his daughter to take care of him. The young woman treated her father with respect and never complained at having to take care of him. Coyote was lucky he had her, but he knew the day would soon come that she would be asked for her hand in marriage and that he would be left alone.

One day, Coyote awoke and summoned his daughter to his bedside. "Daughter dearest, your father is hungry. Go down to the river and see if you might bring something home for me to eat.

But, Daughter, be careful, and keep a watchful eye out for someone who might try to steal you away from me," said Coyote. He knew that she was the most beautiful girl in all the lands and that someone would try to take her.

His daughter obeyed and left immediately for the banks of the great river to hunt for food. Walking along the muddy shores, Coyote's daughter came across five fresh salmon lying in a pile. She thought it strange that someone would just leave such a delicious meal unattended. Suddenly, a handsome young man appeared from out of the water. He was from the Otter tribe.

"These salmon are for you, beautiful daughter of Coyote. I wish to take you for my wife and have you live with me in these waters in peace and happiness for the rest of my days. What do you say?" Otter asked.

"I do not know what to say. I must return to my father and seek his advice in these matters. In a few days, I shall return with an answer for you," she responded.

She took one of the young otter's salmon and returned to her father with her prize. Seeing the salmon, Coyote knew at once that it had been a gift from a suitor, and this angered him. "I will not eat salmon. You must go and find your father the meat of a deer."

Coyote's daughter took the salmon from her father and put it away to eat later herself. The next morning, she gathered up her supplies and left to hunt for her father's supper.

Walking along the same muddy banks where she had encountered the otter, she again saw five salmon in a pile. It was then that the young otter appeared again out of the water.

"Beautiful princess, I have patiently awaited your return and will give to you five fresh salmon again if you accept my proposal of marriage," he said.

"I am afraid, kind Otter, that my father has not given his blessing for the marriage," she answered.

Sad at not having won over the girl, the otter returned to the waters and disappeared. The girl continued to walk along the banks of the river until she came across a pile of the bones of a deer that had been torn apart by wolves. She put them in her basket and carried them back to her father.

"This is good for me. These bones will feed me and revive my strength," said Coyote. "Daughter, I want you to return to the woods and bring me back some more food from this place."

Coyote's daughter was upset that her father had refused the proposal of the handsome otter, but she remained loyal to his wishes and departed the next day to look for more deer meat to satisfy his tastes. Traveling to the same spot where she had found the bones, she came across a deer carcass, but before she could carry it away, five wolves suddenly appeared from the forest. The most handsome of the young wolves fell in love with Coyote's daughter and immediately proposed marriage.

"While I would say yes right now, I must respect the wishes of my father and seek his council," she replied. This was of no worry to the young wolf, for he knew the father must approve of the marriage. So the five wolves helped Coyote's daughter carry the deer to her home. Once there, she cut up the deer, dried its meat and took her prize to her ailing father and told him of the wolf's proposal.

"I consent to the marriage, Daughter. I know that if you are in the care of the wolves, there will always be enough food and you will bring some to your poor father. You must promise to return to see me now and then. I like deer meat. I am Coyote, and I cannot live on salmon alone," he said.

A few days later, Coyote's daughter returned to the place where she had met the wolves, and she found the one who had proposed marriage.

"What was the response from your father?" he asked.

"I have been given permission to wed," she said.

At this, the wolf took his new bride up into the mountains to the village of the Wolf tribe. There was always plenty of dried meat to eat, and all the houses were very big and were adorned with the finest mats and decorations. She was happy in her new life and often returned to her father with enough meat to last him a month. But every time she visited Coyote, she had to walk by the same spot where the young otter had proposed marriage and had been refused. Seeing the happiness on her face made him increasingly angry.

"The Wolf and Coyote clans have embarrassed me, and now I will make trouble for them," said the young otter to himself.

A few days later, Otter went to the village of the wolves. He crept through the shadows of the forest and watched as the wolf and his wife went about their daily chores. He watched as they laughed and prepared their meals together and at night retired to their home to make love and fall asleep. With each passing moment, the young otter's anger grew. He waited until everyone in the village had fallen asleep, then placed logs around the edges of the homes and set them on fire.

Coyote's daughter and her husband tried to jump from their home, but the intense flames pushed them back. They kept trying to escape, but the flames were too strong, and the couple died.

The otter returned to his home in the water, satisfied at having killed the two lovers.

Several days had passed since Coyote had last heard from his daughter, but he thought nothing of it because he had plenty of dried deer meat. Then one day, while Coyote was eating his fill of meat, he heard a voice.

"Father, it is your daughter. My husband and I are on a journey," said the ghostly voice of his daughter. "Join us. I am no longer tied to the earth by flesh, and my body now soars above the clouds. Come and join us in this world so beautiful. If you do not come, I will never be able to see you again."

"Yes, I hear you, Daughter, but how can I join you?" asked Coyote.

"Build a great fire and jump in it. Stay there for a few moments, and you will soon join us in this blissful world," she said.

Coyote did as she said and built a big fire. He jumped into it, but the flames burned his skin, and he jumped right out again. He tried this several more times before giving up.

"Daughter, I cannot join you in your world in this form, for I am bound to earth by flesh."

"You can still visit us. Travel east into the mountains and climb the highest peak. It is there you will find me," said Coyote's daughter.

So Coyote did as she requested and traveled for many days up into the mountains before finally reaching the top of the highest peak just as the sun was about to rise. There, in the early morning light, he saw the shadowy shapes of men and women wandering about, speaking quietly. Coyote ran among them until he finally found his daughter. He was just about to embrace her when the first rays of sun broke over the edge of the earth, and all the spirits of the people disappeared.

Coyote wept at having lost his daughter and remained at the top of the mountain hoping that she might return the next evening. He waited until the sun went down, and sure enough, his daughter appeared before him and he embraced her.

"Dear Daughter, how am I to live on this earth without you? I am now alone, and I carry this grief with me," he said.

"Father, I will never come back to this earth again. We are leaving...," And just as suddenly as she had appeared, she was gone.

Coyote was left on top of the mountain, and for days he remained there, weeping for his daughter. "This sorrow I feel is great. From this day forward,

I will pass on these feelings to humans, and when they lose a loved one, they, too, will know the sorrow of Coyote." It is said that every time a person dies, Coyote can be heard howling his sorrowful tune to the spirits.

# The Creation of the People

AFTER THE GREAT SPIRIT had flooded the world, there was Coyote. It was very lonely for Coyote in the world. He spent most of his days sleeping in the shade during the day and eating the plentiful salmon in the great river. He had done this for many years, when one day, he got bored of his existence.

"Why have I been confined to this world alone? There must be some way to break the bonds of this lonely life?" he thought.

So Coyote traveled across all the lands, looking for someone he could talk with, just to find anyone so that he would know that he wasn't alone in the world. Coyote traveled south through mountains and deserts, through jungles and grasslands, but could find no one. He then traveled to the north, braving the cold winds and blowing snow only to find the landscape barren of life. Coyote then headed east until he could go no farther, and still he found no one to call a friend. Therefore, Coyote returned to the land of the great river to live his life in eternal solitude.

Then one day Coyote had a thought. "Why don't I create the first tribes of people?" Coyote spent many days thinking about what exactly to create. There never had been people on the earth, so Coyote did not know what they should look like. He created a mold of how he thought the people would look and filled it with mud, rocks, moss and a drop of his own blood. Placing the mold over the fire to bake, Coyote became very tired from all the work and fell asleep. He awoke to the acrid smell of his creation burning over the fire, and when he pulled the figure from its mold, he looked down and saw that he had created Black Fly. It flew into the air, bit Coyote's neck and tasted his blood. From that day on, Black Fly had a taste for blood and would bite its victims because it was angry for what Coyote had done to it.

Frustrated at his failure but still determined to create the people, Coyote mixed in moss, mud, the branches of a giant cedar and a single tear. Coyote then put his new mold over the fire to cure and watched it very carefully. Thinking it was done, he picked up the hot mold with his bare hands and burned himself. He tossed the mold in the air and out flew Eagle. Eagle was taken out of the fire too early, however, and that is the reason why Eagle's body was baked a golden brown, and the uncooked part, his head, remains white. Angry over not having been fully cooked, Eagle did not stay close to Coyote and refused to become his friend.

Coyote broke his mold in anger, but he did not give up trying. For many days, he tried new molds and new ingredients, but he could not create the people. He made Buffalo, Mole, Deer and Grizzly Bear, but he still could not come up with a mold good enough for the people.

Coyote searched across the world for the proper mold and ingredients, eventually creating all the world's animals as they are today, but he still had no luck in finding the right combination. The Great Spirit had been watching over Coyote's work with curiosity, and one day he paid Coyote a visit.

Coyote had never seen the Great Spirit and could not help but be amazed by his appearance. The Great Spirit had only two legs on which to stand, yet he did not fall over, his torso was long and muscular, and his head, the strangest part of all, was round. The Great Spirit did not have any fur, feathers or scales like all the other animals, but only glowing red skin that had been kissed by the sun.

"Coyote, I have watched over you these many years, and I am pleased with your creations. Why do you look so sad and forlorn when you have filled the earth with many beautiful creatures?" asked the Great Spirit.

"Wise Chief, although I am content with the animals, they are just too stupid for me. Their only concern is survival, therefore they spend most of their days trying to find something to eat and then sleeping in the shade. My intellect is second only to your own, so I need someone with whom I might interact with every day," said Coyote.

The Great Spirit then handed Coyote a sack filled with ingredients and said, "You will make a mold in my image and then fill it with the ingredients in the sack. But be warned, you will have to watch it very carefully while it cures over the flames."

Coyote thanked the Great Spirit for his help, and then in a bright flash of light, the Great Spirit disappeared. Coyote set out right away to create the people in the Great Spirit's image. He made a new mold in his form and poured in a portion of the ingredients. He stirred the mixture together, and when he added a little bit of water, it turned as white as snow. Then Coyote placed the mold over the fire and watched it carefully. Not wanting to fail, Coyote took the mold off a little too early, and when he looked down at the mold, the person he had created was still white. Coyote was so angry for having made another error that he picked up the mold and threw it with all his strength toward the eastern horizon.

"I will try one more time, and if I fail, I will give up my pursuit of trying to create the people," said Coyote.

So again he poured the last remaining ingredients from the sack into the mold, added water and mixed it all together. With great care, Coyote placed the mold over the fire and tended to it as if it was his child. When he deemed the mold ready, he removed it from the fire and placed it on the ground to cool in the breeze. When Coyote finally looked upon his creation, he said, "These will be the people created in the image of the Great Spirit."

This is why the people have always been in these lands, for Coyote created them in the image of the Great Spirit and placed them along the great rivers and mountain valleys.

# The Visitors

GENERATIONS PASSED, AND the people lived their lives in peace and prosperity. It is often told by the elders that long ago, before there were humans, there was Coyote, and one day, he decided to create the people. It was said that our people were created in the image of the Great Spirit and that they were given this land as his chosen ones. All the people know this truth, but among the elders they spoke of another people created by Coyote that lived in a far-off land. It was said that because the Great Spirit did not favor them, they were cursed with skin as pale as the snow and an empty space within their spirit that could not be filled. But as the generations passed, the stories became just that—tales of a time long passed that became nothing more than entertainment for children. Life went on, and the ancient times were forgotten.

Then one day, in a village by the river, came whispers from the east of visitors to the lands. Hunters spoke of other tribes coming into contact with a people who spoke in a strange tongue, who wore odd-looking clothing and had skin as white as the clouds. At first, the people thought these were just stories, as the forests could sometimes play tricks on the mind, but when a group of hunters passing through the village showed an elder some metal implements and strange clothing taken from the strangers, a council was immediately called.

"I pray you, noble men, remember the stories you were once told as young ones," said the chief of the village to the local elders. "I remember sitting with my grandfather and listening to him tell of a people from a far-off land. He would tell me of their pale faces and their strange ways. I always thought they were just stories to scare children, but it appears the myths were true."

Listening outside through a small gap in the lodge was the curious young son of the chief, Gasga. He had heard these same stories all his life, but he had always believed in the pale-faced people, and unlike most of the others, he did not fear them. Gasga listened as his father and the elders discussed what would be done upon the arrival of these visitors. Some of the elders spoke of war, some spoke of retreat and others wanted to greet them as friends.

"Must we provoke war with a people we do not know? By all the items they have been trading with the hunters, they seem to be a powerful people, so maybe we can learn from them and welcome them here," said the chief.

"But all that they desire is to lay claim to this land. Why have they left their homes to come to ours? It is because they seek to claim what is not theirs?" protested one untrusting elder.

"We must make a show of force!" cried another. "Slaughter them and show no mercy, and they will run away, never to return."

It was then that Gasga burst into the room and spoke his mind to the council. "How can you fear that which you do not know? The strange, pale-faced people have come a long way, and we can't simply cut them down. We must learn from them, and maybe it will benefit our tribe," said Gasga with passion in his voice.

"Young one," said his father, "you cannot come in here and expect your voice to be heard by the council."

"But..."

"This is not your place. But your words do not fall upon deaf ears. If the people of light skin have come from far off, then they will not likely be returning easily. Although we do not know their motives, we cannot simply kill them and expect them to go away. If they are indeed a people with powers, then we must try to understand them," said the chief. "Son, since you have shown interest and are the bravest of our young men, I will send you out to meet with these visitors and learn their ways. Though my heart is heavy that you will depart into uncertainty, this is your choice. You will experience new things along the way, and some might be dangerous, but go with a warrior's mind and carry your people in your heart."

For two days, the chief and Gasga prepared for the young man's voyage, gathering supplies and speaking of the obstacles and dangers that he might face. The chief did not take this decision lightly to send his only son, because if he could not send Gasga into the unknown, then how could he send someone else's child? But they needed to know what the visitors wanted and if they came in peace.

"Son, I want you to be on guard out there and remember that the motives of men are not always good. I thought the stories I heard as a child were just stories, and now that the pale-skinned ones are a reality, I wonder what parts of those tales will come true next," said the chief to his son as he departed the village.

Gasga walked out into the wild and headed east. He spent his days along the path thinking about the wonders he might discover. The stories he had heard throughout his life ran through his head. Some stories told of the pale-faced people with mystical powers, some tales spoke of them as vicious demons who had been cast out of their lands on the moon. Other stories talked of Coyote creating an incomplete people and banishing them to a land on the other side of the earth. The legends might have predicted their existence, but that did not mean they came with other motives. He was hopeful his encounter would be a positive one.

Gasga found a good spot in the forest and built himself a camp for the night. He awoke the next day and traveled east for some distance before coming to a village of the tribe of the far eastern valleys. He knew the people were proud and strong, but what he came across did not match his expectations. A strange silence hung over the village as he approached. From a distance, he could see that no one was moving about. Fire pits burned but no one sat by them, and mangy dogs ran about sniffing at the ground. The sun was just falling behind the mountains, and a chill passed over the young man as he entered the village.

The scene he walked into was one of horror. There were people in this village, but they were not well. He saw an old man lying in front of his home and approached him. The old man stared directly into the eyes of the young man but did not see him. Gasga tried to speak to him, but the old man did not respond, only muttering words under his breath in a language he could not understand. As he searched through the village, Gasga came upon more people lying prostrate on the ground with sweat pouring down their faces, muttering through chattering teeth. It was nothing like he had ever seen or heard of. Children lay dead in the streets alongside their mothers as if they had been dumped onto the ground.

"This must be the work of an evil spirit," Gasga thought. "It has to be."

Pushing through the doors to the home of the chief of the village, the young man could not see anyone in the fading light but could hear someone laboring for each breath. In a dark corner on the floor, he found the chief of the village. He lay wrapped in blankets, shivering by a dying fire.

"Honorable Chief, what has happened to your people? What evil has cursed you?" asked the young man.

The chief turned his head toward the young man, looked on him with vacant eyes and spoke in a whisper. "They...demons everywhere.... no hope..." Then his eyes closed, and his spirit joined those of his ancestors. Gasga did not know what to make of this. He could not imagine what sort of force could do this to an entire village, but the words of the dying chief still echoed through his mind. What could have destroyed this once-vibrant village? The chief said he had seen "demons everywhere." The people did not seem like they had prepared or fought in a battle but had been caught off guard by something. Gasga could not stand to look upon the bodies. Since he could do nothing for the people, he left them and headed back onto the path, trying to forget the horror he had witnessed.

For several more days, Gasga walked through the steep mountain passes and deep valleys before finally arriving at the flat plains of the east. In the distance, he spotted a settlement and a plume of smoke rising from a fire. But this did not look like any other settlement he had ever seen. The people were dressed in the strangest clothing. As he got closer, he knew he had finally found the visitors.

For two days, he watched the camp from afar, learning whatever he could about the strangers' daily life. He watched as they prepared their meals, washed their clothes in the river and bedded down for the night. These could not be the same people the stories had spoken of, for they seemed to be just people. Indeed they were different than his tribe, but they did not look like they carried demons inside. He decided to make his presence known and meet the visitors.

Gasga thought that he and the visitors would not be able to speak to each other, but one of them spoke a broken dialect similar to his own language. A man wearing a black robe with a white collar welcomed him into the camp. Gasga marveled at all the things that the visitors had—so many things he had never even seen before, and he had no idea what they did. He spent the night talking with the man in the black robe and learned many new things. The man, a sort of shaman of the visitors, told him of the far-away lands they had come from and the many wonders found there. Gasga did not understand why his people had long told stories about the visitors being bad people. Coyote had simply not mixed his ingredients properly.

These newcomers were strange, indeed. Gasga watched as the pale-faced ones took small sticks from their pockets, placed them in their mouths and put fire to the end. He was amazed when white smoke emerged from their mouths. He thought that they would surely burn up from the inside, but they were unharmed. Gasga thought that the strangers must have the powers of the spirit world within them to survive.

One of the young pale-faced men then pulled out some big sticks to show Gasga. Gasga watched as the man filled the stick with a strange-looking powder and packed it down with another stick. The pale-faced man then set up a basket at one end of a field and the stood some distance away pointing the big stick directly at the basket. Gasga could not figure out what the pale one was doing, but all of a sudden, a loud bang issued forth from the end of the stick along with a plume of white smoke. Gasga thought that surely these people of the white skin knew great magic.

For days, Gasga lived among the small group of visitors before he was taken to meet their chief. He was asked if a few men could follow him back to his home along with their shaman so that they might trade with them and learn of their ways. Their chief assured Gasga that they just wanted to trade with his people, exchanging their metal pots, weapons and blankets for the pelts of animals. Gasga could not understand why they wanted so many pelts, but he was eager to return home and prove to his father that he had succeeded.

After traveling west with the man in the black robe and two others helping to carry goods, Gasga finally arrived in his native lands and the village of his father's tribe. The people of the village were frightened at the appearance of the mythical pale-skinned people, but when they saw the young chief's son with them, their fears passed. A great feast was prepared, but the chief did not participate. He remained wary of the visitors' intentions when his son told him of the numbers of them in the east. Gasga tried to assuage his father's fears, saying that the pale-faced ones had come only to trade items, but the chief did not yet trust them.

"These white men appear normal, but something does not fit, my son," the chief said to Gasga one evening. "They come with smiling faces, but their motives are hidden. I do not trust them."

The visitors remained in the village for several weeks, trading items for furs and exchanging stories with the people. Despite the air of peace throughout the village, things quickly changed. The people began to cough, the young fell ill and some of the elders died mysteriously. Gasga had seen this before. The pale-faced ones, however, did not fall ill and watched idly by as more of the people died. Gasga pleaded with the pale-faced visitors, but they would not help. He knew then that the visitors were the carriers of the demons his people now held inside.

"It was you who did this to us!" the young man cried out to the man in the black robe.

"These lands will belong to us one day. More of our people will come. There are many riches to be had here, and many men will come to seek their fortunes. The way of the red man is fading. You have shown us the way through the mountains, and more of us will return. Those of you who do not bend to our demands will perish," said the man in the black robe.

It wasn't long before Gasga fell ill with a demon in his spirit, and all but a handful of his people did not die. The young man retired to his lodge to lay down, and until he drew his last breath, all he could whisper was, "They...demons everywhere... no hope..."

Generations passed, and more of the white-faced visitors came, and more of the people died. Those created in the image of the Great Spirit still cling to their bits of land and await the coming of Coyote and the Great One to return the earth to balance.

# The Sweat Lodge

WHEN THE WORLD WAS first created, the Great Spirit made all the animals and gave them names. He made a huge, fierce beast with large teeth and dagger-like claws and named it Grizzly Bear. He then made an animal with a muscular body, lean legs and a head adorned with antlers and named it Deer.

The Great Spirit thus created all the animals on earth. And then he created Coyote, and although he didn't have much muscle and wasn't blessed with the power of flight, Coyote was given the power of intellect and named chief of all the animal tribes. When he had finished creating all the creatures of the animal kingdom, the Great Spirit made human beings and scattered them all across the lands. As he looked down upon his creation from the sky, the Great Spirit thought something was missing to make the world a paradise for those that lived on it. Everything looked to be in perfect order, but the creatures of the earth walked about in a fog. The Great Spirit watched as all the people wandered about night and day, never at peace and unable to understand their purpose in the world. He observed the people for several days before asking his wife to look down upon his creation and see what was missing. Instantly, she saw the problem.

"There is no place for the animal people and the human beings to cleanse their minds, their bodies and their souls," said the wife of the Great Spirit. She then summoned Coyote to her side and gave him a task. "Dear Coyote, the creatures of the earth wander about in a daze and do not enjoy all the wonders that the Great Spirit has provided," she said. She then reached inside her chest and pulled out a piece of her rib and handed it to Coyote. "Take my rib and use its pieces to create a sweat lodge," she instructed.

She was glad to help Coyote in this task that would give the people a place to cleanse their bodies and pray to the spirits for strength, health and happiness. These are the essential needs of the people, and without them, they would continue to walk the earth as they would in the land of the dead.

"But remember what I tell you. The sweat lodge will be a sacred place in which my spirit will dwell, and if it is not taken care of, the creatures of the earth will feel my vengeance," warned the wife of the Great Spirit. She then gave Coyote specific instructions on how to build the sweat lodge.

After listening to her, Coyote traveled down from the sky and called a council of all the tribal chiefs. From far and wide the noble chiefs of the tribes descended on the home of Coyote for the hastily called council meeting. Coyote watched as the Eagle chief arrived from out of the sky and the Salmon chief left his home in the river and walked on land, and the humans also sent their chief to listen to the proclamations of Coyote.

"Coyote, you had better have called us all here for a reason," announced the Eagle chief. "My people fly about the skies with no direction, for their minds have been clouded by something."

"I promise you that all your problems will soon disappear. It is the wish of the Great Spirit's wife that the people of the earth have a place to retire from the world and to cleanse their minds and souls of the stresses of daily life. She called it the sweat lodge, and she has given me instructions for how to build it."

Coyote then pulled out the rib belonging to the wife of the Great Spirit and showed it to the chiefs, who now believed Coyote's words.

"But listen carefully now," said Coyote, "because there are strict rules to follow when building a sweat lodge. Watch me closely as I construct one so that you may learn and spread this knowledge to your people."

Coyote broke the rib bone into several pieces and began to put together the sweat lodge.

"To build the frame of the lodge, I am going to use the rib from the Great Spirit's wife, but for everyone on earth, use the young branches of a fir or birch tree, for their flexibility and strength will make it easy to construct a proper foundation. Be sure to build this frame low to the ground so that people will have to bow to enter the lodge, and this will also ensure that the steam will remain close to their bodies. The frame can then be covered with bark, grass and earth to retain the healing steam.

"Next, you will heat stones in a fire just outside of the lodge. Carefully roll the stones into the lodge and close the entranceway. Once inside the lodge, place the stones in the center and pour cold water over them. Hot steam will then fill the area. Try to remain seated in the lodge for an hour or more, with short breaks in between. This will give your body time to cleanse itself, and your mind will release the stresses of the day. While sitting in the lodge, you may sing songs in praise of the Great Spirit's wife and pray each time someone enters or leaves the lodge. If proper respect is not paid to the sweat lodge and to the sacrifice the Great Spirit's wife has made by giving us this gift, then the people will become ill. When you leave the sweat lodge, do not discard the stones, as they can be used over and over again. These are the instructions that were handed down to me by the Great Spirit and his wife. Follow them and our people shall be rewarded, for the sweat lodge is a place of healing and enlightenment. Stray from them and sickness will follow. Now return to your people and spread this good news."

The chief of all the tribes of peoples on earth departed from Coyote's home and returned to teach the people how to use the sweat lodge. After one session in the sweat lodge, the people emerged from their daze and could finally open their eyes to the world around them. The change was immediate. The souls of the people were lifted to new heights, and from his house in the sky, the Great Spirit saw that the people on earth had found peace.

Whenever the people entered their sweat lodge, they offered up prayers to the wife of the Great Spirit for having given them this gift. They used the lodge when people felt unwell, and it cured their illness. They used it when they had injured themselves, and their wounds healed. They used the lodge before embarking on the hunt to purify their souls and clear their minds of all distractions. Each time they entered the lodge, they sang:

*Spirit of the sweat lodge hear my call,*
*Open my soul and cleanse my mind.*
*Once we walked stupid and blind,*
*Into those days never again will we fall.*

For many years, the people followed the instructions of Coyote, and all was well until one day a young boy broke the rules of the sweat lodge and offended the wife of the Great Spirit. Angered at not being able to heat the stones properly, the impatient youth kicked the stones about and damaged the frame of the lodge. Just a few moments later, he was struck down with incredible pains and was ill for many weeks. When others in the village learned what the boy had done, they gathered in the sweat lodge and asked forgiveness for the boy's behavior. After a few days, the boy recovered, and he never again angered the sweat lodge spirit.

# The End

FOR MILLENNIA, COYOTE ROAMED the world seeing to his works. He conquered the great beasts of the plains, killed the monster serpents of the waters and turned the giants of the mountains into many of the harmless creatures of the world today. When the Great Spirit in his wisdom saw fit to bring the people into the world, Coyote helped them to survive. He showed them how to use language and how to build their villages, and when they were hungry, Coyote even led the salmon up the river so the people could eat. While the people were still young and finding their way through the world, they would often call out to Coyote when they needed help, but as time passed, he heard fewer prayers in his name. The people had learned what they needed and began to spread out from their place of birth into the valleys and onto the distant plains.

But as much as Coyote had helped the people to survive in the world, he was a jealous and shifty character known to play evil tricks on the Great Spirit's chosen people. Village after village could recount thousands of stories of times when Coyote had come and brought misery and unhappiness to the population simply for his own amusement. He had become such a nuisance in some villages that many no longer beseeched Coyote for his help as they feared his trickery.

Coyote traveled from one village to another, waiting to answer the prayers of the people, but none ever came.

"People somewhere must need me. I will travel far across all the known lands to find some amusement," Coyote said into the wind.

The next morning, Coyote left his home and set out in search of a village or even just a single person who needed him and had not heard of his deceitful ways. For weeks, Coyote traveled through thick forests and along the great riverbanks searching for someone who might call out to him in need, someone who might need the powerful magic of the Coyote spirit.

After several days of walking under the blistering sun, Coyote was on the point of collapsing and giving up on his quest. Luckily, he happened upon a large freshwater lake, which he immediately ran into, drinking the cold liquid for nearly an hour. He was so involved in the slaking of his thirst that he failed to notice a village on the other side of the lake.

"Finally, after days under the oppression of the sun, I have found a people who can use my unique services. For I am Coyote, and I am strong," he said with confidence.

Just as Coyote stepped out of the water and back onto the shore, he heard a noise coming from the darkness through the trees. A twig snapped under the weight of the intruder, and Coyote called out to the mysterious presence.

"Who goes there, sneaking up on the great Coyote?" he called out.

A voice answered from the cover of the woods, "You will not find anyone for you to swindle, Coyote."

"Come out, stranger, and explain your words. How do you know my intentions?" replied Coyote.

His eyes grew wide with fear when he saw the face of a great black bear emerge from the darkness of the forest. Coyote had tamed many a beast in his days on earth, but the members of the Bear clan were just too powerful for his magic.

"I know you well, Coyote, and when you spoke of your intentions to find amusement, the wind carried your words across the lands for all to hear," said Black Bear, walking up to Coyote.

"Nonsense. The people could not have heard my words. Besides, my cunning knows no match, so surely I will find some place to entertain my every whim. My name might precede me, but these lesser beings know nothing of my powers. I will prove you wrong, Bear," replied Coyote.

"Don't take my warnings to mean that I care. You have spent an eternity in this world using it as your personal playground. There will come a time when you are no longer needed, and that time is soon at hand. You have done the Great Spirit's work, and when your actions are no longer needed, he will come in search of you," said Black Bear before disappearing once again into the cover of the forest shadows.

Angry at hearing Black Bear's words, Coyote screamed into the shadows, "Foolish Bear, if you think I cannot find one mere mortal in the world who will not fall for my charms, you are mistaken, for my powers are great and unending."

Leaving the edge of the lake, Coyote began walking toward the village off in the distance. He would prove to Black Bear and to the Great Spirit that he was still needed in the world by the people and that he could use his power to make them believe they needed him.

As Coyote approached the entrance to the village, he was immediately greeted by one of the elders of the community. The people did not recognize him as the great Coyote spirit because he had cleverly disguised himself in the form of a man from a neighboring village.

"What brings you to this poor village, stranger? We would normally welcome you with a great feast and many days of celebration, but the hunt has not provided as in previous years, and many of our women and children go without their daily rations. You may enter and share some dried salmon with us," said the elder, leading the disguised Coyote into the main lodging.

Once inside, a portion of dried salmon was brought in for the traveler by the one of the elder's daughters. She was the most beautiful woman Coyote had ever seen. It was then that he came up with a plan.

"My dearest hosts, I know of a way to get more food than you could possibly need. I will show you this way if you will give me this beautiful woman in exchange," said Coyote to the village elder.

The proposal took the elder by surprise, and he quietly thought it over. Coyote sat before the elder but did not take his lustful eyes off the woman he desired.

"I have thought over your proposal, stranger, and we are not a people who are easily fooled," said the elder, who stood up abruptly and threw a magic powder over the guest, who instantly revealed his true form.

"How did you guess that it was me?" asked Coyote.

"I have been on this earth long enough to have heard the tales of your trickery, and although you promise great things and my people are in need, the price you ask is too high," the elder proudly exclaimed. "Many praises to you, noble spirit, but we can find our way in the world. We have come through difficult times in the past and will survive the future."

Annoyed at the turn of events, Coyote turned to leave. "You are a lot wiser than you look, Elder. I have given many things to your people, and you have turned your back on me. The day will come when you will need my help, and I just might not answer," he said.

Storming out of the lodge, Coyote ran away from the village, ashamed at having been discovered so easily, but he was armed with even more resolve to prove his powers to the mortals of the world.

Coyote again began his journey and came upon many villages, but the people continually turned him away. "It seems that my reputation precedes me," lamented Coyote. He had almost given up hope when he came across an old man walking along the same path. But what Coyote mistook for a helpless old man was in fact the Great Spirit in disguise.

Coyote managed to jump off the path before the old man had noticed him taking cover behind a row of bushes. "This old man surely does not know who I am. I will disguise myself as an old man and surprise him with an incredible display of power and skills that he will never expect and that will surely bring me renown across all the lands."

Transforming into an old man, Coyote slowly emerged from behind the bushes and called out to the other traveler on the path. After the two exchanged greetings, Coyote immediately began to describe all the wonderful things he had accomplished in his long life—all the beasts he had killed, all the mountains he had traversed and all the magic he had performed. For nearly an hour, Coyote told wondrous tales of his exploits and of all the people he had fooled using his superior cunning. The old man simply stood and listened to Coyote's words without uttering a single sound until he had finished, at which point he burst into a mocking laughter that was echoed by a group of ravens perched in a nearby tree. Coyote hung his head in shame at yet again failing to impress one of the Great Spirit's mortal creations.

"With powers great as yours, you must surely be the one called Coyote, for no one else can perform such feats," said the old man.

"Yes, I am the Coyote of legend. Why then do you mock my legendary feats?" asked Coyote.

"If you are indeed Coyote and are as powerful as you boast, then you can do just about anything that I command," replied the old man.

Eager to finally show one person that he was still of value, Coyote agreed to the request. Coyote transformed back into his original form and readied himself for the old man's tasks.

"For your first test, I want you to take that river and change its course," said the old man, pointing off the path to a raging river.

"Your task does not worry me one bit, for I am all powerful," said Coyote, who then waved his hands over the torrential waters. Coyote's face strained at the effort of reversing such a powerful current, but soon the waters began to churn, almost appearing to boil. With great effort, Coyote waved his hands one last time, suddenly calming the waters. The old man walked to the river's edge and saw that Coyote had indeed changed the course of the river.

"Impressive, but I am not yet convinced," said the old man. "I want you now to move that mountain and place it in the valley just ahead of us."

"Old man, how can you doubt my powers after I have reversed the flow of this mighty river? What more proof do you need that I am all powerful?" pleaded Coyote.

"If you are Coyote, then this should be easy for you," taunted the old man.

"Just stand aside and watch a god do his work," exclaimed Coyote proudly.

Taking a deep breath, Coyote strained his magical powers to their limits trying to move the mountain from its foundation. But through the calm of the day, the ground suddenly shook, trees trembled from roots to tips and the creatures ran for cover. The mountain shook violently and lifted into the air as dirt and rocks fell to the ground. Wide-eyed, Coyote strained under the pressure of holding up the mountain but found he could not move it to the location the old man had indicated.

"I don't know what is happening!" yelled Coyote.

THE END

Coyote could not move the mountain because the old man, the Great Spirit, had willed it not to move. Coyote tried to muster all the strength he had, but the Great Spirit simply would not allow the mountain to be relocated.

Exhausted, Coyote looked at the old man and knew at once who this stranger was. "Since I cannot move this mountain any farther, there must be a greater magic other than my own working against me. I can only say that you must be the Great Spirit come to test me," said Coyote.

"You have seen through my disguise, Coyote," said the old man, who, with a simple thought, placed the mountain back in its place. "I have watched you for sometime now wandering this existence looking for purpose. You were placed on this earth at the very beginning and have done many great things. But lately, you have become listless and have become something of a nuisance to the people of this land. They have taken your lessons and are surviving in this world. The time has come for you to leave this earth. I am returning to the heavens soon, and you will be coming with me on this journey."

"But I have not finished my works," pleaded Coyote. "The people of this world are still young and could use my guidance."

"The people of this world may indeed be young, but they have firm roots," scolded the Great Spirit. "I have seen your works, and although you say you have helped the people, your methods leave much to be desired. Therefore, we will leave this world to the people and only come back to wipe the earth clean and start again."

"I accept my fate, Great Spirit, and will do as you command," said Coyote.

With that, the Great Spirit built a house of ice and stone on the highest mountain. Coyote's only companion for his long slumber would be a small fire that would burn throughout eternity until he would reawaken.

It has long been said that every time Coyote turns in his sleep, summer blossoms, and winter's chill descends when he rolls over to the other side of his bed. So it is in this state that Coyote remains to this day, sleeping in front of that fire, waiting for the Great Spirit to call upon him to make his glorious return to earth when the people need him once again.